You, _____,
will find in these messages the daily encouragement
to continue in the pursuit of your dreams.

Something to

SMILE
About

Encouragement

and Inspiration for Life's

UPS and DOWNS

ZIG ZIGLAR

OLIVER
NELSON

THOMAS NELSON PUBLISHERS
Nashville • Atlanta • London • Vancouver

Published in Nashville, Tennessee, by Thomas Nelson, Inc.

Scripture quotations noted NKJV are from THE NEW KING JAMES VERSION. Copyright © 1979, 1980, 1982, Thomas Nelson, Inc., Publishers. Scripture quotations noted KJV are from the King James Version of the Bible.

Library of Congress Cataloging-in-Publication Data

Ziglar, Zig.
    Something to smile about : encouragement and inspiration for life's ups and downs / Zig Ziglar.
        p.   cm.
    ISBN 0-8407-9183-6
    1. Conduct of life—Anecdotes. 2. Success—Anecdotes.
I. Title.
BJ1581.2.Z54   1997
158—dc21   97-18631
                                        CIP

Printed in the United States of America.

12 — 02 01

To Bernie Lofchick, "Brother Bern," the most positive person I know and a constant source of encouragement. He believed in me before I believed in myself.

Contents

Foreword   *xi*

Introduction   *xiii*

Follow the Leader—If   *1*

Ambition—Good or Bad?   *3*

From Sharecropper's Daughter to College President   *5*

The Power of the Word   *7*

Appearance Counts   *9*

Why Worry?   *11*

Tying Your Shoes   *13*

Leaders Accept Responsibility   *15*

Prevention—The Best "Cure" for Addiction   *17*

The Bounce-Back Kid   *19*

The Power of Attitude   *21*

Leaders Are Managers   *23*

Doing Beats Talking Every Time   *25*

He's Eighty-Five But Who's Counting?   *27*

Get To or Got To?   *29*

Why Not Use What Works?   *31*

Making the Ball Bounce Your Way   *33*

Leadership That Leads   *35*

The Choice Is Yours   *37*

His Commitment Was Total   *39*

Conviction Is the Key   *41*

Motivation, Manipulation, and Leadership   *43*

It's in the Heart   45

Miss Amy Whittington Is a Difference Maker   47

The Dignity of Simplicity   49

The Little Town That Could   51

Respond—Don't React   53

Truth Is Stranger and More Exciting Than Fiction   55

Intelligent Selfishness   57

". . . To Keep Myself . . ."   59

It's Never Too Late!   61

Out of the Ashes   63

Employability   65

Work—Who Needs It?   67

The Entrepreneur Is Alive and Well   69

Leaders Are Communicators   71

Moving Up in Life   73

How to Finish Well   75

Help Others—Help Yourself   77

Friends   79

She Drew the Line   81

Love Says No to the Moment   83

Getting Even   85

This Is a Philosophy, Not a Tactic   87

"What I Do Is Who I Am"   89

The Ten-Year-Old Entrepreneur   91

Manners Do Matter   93

This Way to Happiness   95

Life Is Like a Grindstone   97

Needed—One More Friend   99

My Most Unforgettable Character   101
It's Not Where You Start—It's Where You Go   103
One Incident Can Change Us Forever   105
Improbable, Impossible, and Can't Happen   107
Do Long Hours Guarantee More Productivity and
     More Profit?   109
The Fully Equipped Cow   111
Reward Yourself   113
Be Kind and Listen   115
Inspiring Teachers Produce Inspired Students   117
Reading, Writing, and Arithmetic—Not Enough   119
She Gave Everything She Had   121
One Basket at a Time   123
Part-Timer Makes It Big-Time   125
It's Better to Give   127
It's Not My Fault   129
Let's Hear It for Brenda Reyes and the Marine Corps   131
Little Things Do Make Big Differences   133
I'm the Only One Who Does Anything Around Here!   135
A Team of All-Stars or an All-Star Team?   137
Revitalizing Older Citizens   139
From Wealth to Broke to Wealth   141
Those "Instant" Successes   143
Love Is a Score in Tennis   145
"She Was Speed and Motion Incarnate"   147
All of Us Are in Debt   149
Sam Walton Was a People Person   151
Is There More Than One Way?   153

Persistence Really Does Pay   155
Anything Can Happen—And It Often Does   157
Big Events Don't Always Get Big Attention   159
Win-Win Negotiations   161
". . . To Help Other People . . ."   163
Respond or React   165
St. John's—A College That Works   167
Be Grateful for Your Problems   169
How Old Are You?   171
Good News in the Newspaper   173
"Don't Give It a Thought"   175
Be a Good-Finder   177
Stress—Good or Bad?   179
He Got Better, Not Bitter   181
K.I.S.S.   183
Success Is a Partnership   185
The Edsel Was an Outstanding Success   187
Turning Tragedy into Triumph   189
Yesterday's Impossibles   191
Eating an Elephant   193
It Takes Courage   195
If the Decision Is Wrong, Change It   197
It's Not What You Don't Have   199
Learn to Say Yes   201
Is It a Problem or an Opportunity?   203
About the Author   205

Foreword

Dr. Buckner Fanning points out that a parable is a short story with a long meaning. He shares this parable, taken directly from Charles Schulz's "Peanuts" comic strip. The first frame shows a dark night, and Snoopy is in the doghouse. He goes to Charlie Brown's front door and kicks it. Charlie Brown looks out the window and says, "Are you feeling lonely again?" In the next frame Charlie Brown and Snoopy are walking together, and Charlie Brown says to Snoopy, "It's a terrible feeling, isn't it?" In the next frame they are both in bed, covers pulled up, as Charlie Brown is obviously trying to comfort his depressed companion, saying, "You wake up in the middle of the night and everything seems hopeless. You're all alone." Snoopy pulls the covers even higher. Charlie Brown says, "You wonder what life is all about and why you're here. Does anyone really care? And you just stare into the dark and feel all alone." In the final frame Snoopy looks at Charlie Brown and longingly asks, "Do we have any night cookies?"

From time to time all of us need some "night cookies." The purpose of this book is to give you some night cookies and persuade you to pass them on to others. Night cookies are essentially lifters or pleasant interludes that are difference makers in people's lives. *The American Dictionary of the English Language, Noah Webster 1828* (which I'll refer to several times in this book by the phrase "the 1828 Noah Webster dictionary"), defines *difference* as "the state of being unlike or distinct; the quality which distinguishes one thing from another."

It is a "logical distinction." *Distinct* means "different, not the same." Logically, we could say it is an essential attribute. A *maker* is "one who shapes, forms or molds," so a difference maker is one who makes a distinct difference in another by shaping, forming, molding, or influencing.

Sometimes you make a difference in unexpected and unexplained ways. As you read these parables and their applications, you will frequently find yourself saying, "If he can, I can too," "If she can, so can I." That's the first step in becoming a difference maker.

I love the story of the sociology class that studied 200 young boys, most of whom came from the inner city in Baltimore, Maryland. As a result of their study the students came to the same conclusion for each of the boys: "He hasn't got a chance." Twenty-five years later another sociology professor did a follow-up study and was able to locate 180 of the original 200 boys. Of that number, 176 had become doctors, lawyers, successful businessmen, etc. When the question was asked of the men how they had been able to escape their predicted future, they all, in one way or another, said basically the same thing: "There was this teacher . . ." The professor found the teacher and asked her what she had done to have such an impact on so many of the boys. She simply smiled and said, "I just loved those boys."

My hope is that through this book, you will experience vicariously the love of a number of people as I relate their stories and what they have meant to so many. If you apply what you experience and share your story with me, there is a chance a future book will feature your story.

Introduction

I have several specific objectives for this book. First, as the title clearly states, it is to give you a daily word of encouragement, which is the fuel of hope. It will also give you something to smile about and, on occasion, even a healthy laugh. Each page is designed to fill a need that you might have, not necessarily today but at some point in your life.

Companies can use pages from this book to hold short sales meetings, staff meetings, or department meetings. At these short get-togethers, someone can either read or explain the material, and ideas can be exchanged about how the concepts apply to their situation. Husbands and wives can read the book to each other over breakfast or dinner and draw closer to each other. Parents can use it as a guideline or motivation for their children. Teachers can share the book with their classes, while some businesses might make copies available to every employee. People from all walks of life can share favorite passages with friends or family who need an encouraging word. In short, there are many ways these messages can be used to encourage you and others.

In a world that is too negative, it's my conviction that we need something daily to overcome the negatives. I believe you will find encouragement here that will make a difference in your life.

I invite you not to read this book, but to dissect it page by page. I suggest you keep your pen handy and mark the specific thoughts and ideas contained herein. Then when you have an occasion to use a story, example, illustration, or joke, your memory bank will be prepared to find what you need.

The last thoughts we put into our minds before we go to sleep definitely influence us. So, just before you go to sleep at night, read and concentrate on one of the messages. If you have been watching the evening news, you would do well to read several pages and contemplate what you have read before you turn the lights out.

Follow the Leader—If

I'll be the first to admit that sheep are not the most intelligent creatures on earth, but from time to time I wonder about some of us people. When sheepherders wish to move their flock from one pasture to another, if there is a slight obstacle in the path, they let a goat lead the way, and it will be the first to jump over the obstacle. The sheep follow dutifully. Interestingly enough, you could remove the obstacle, and the sheep would continue to jump over an obstacle that no longer exists.

To a degree, people are the same way. A major cross-country race in Kuala Lumpur, Malaysia, was to cover a seven-mile course. Two hours after the race began, there were no runners in sight, and the officials became concerned that something had happened. They set out in their automobiles to find the runners and discovered that all were six or more miles away, running in the wrong direction. Some had actually covered more than ten miles. A. J. Rogers, a race official, said the mix-up apparently occurred when the runner leading the pack took a wrong turn at the fifth checkpoint and the rest followed him.

> *Experience is a hard teacher. It gives the test first, the lesson afterward.*

John Maxwell from San Diego, California, says that in a lifetime, the average person directly or indirectly influences ten thousand other people. Those who are in leadership positions influence many, many more. That's the reason leadership carries such an incredible responsibility—namely, that of making certain you're heading in the right direction, that the decisions you make are character-based and the route you choose is a good one. When you make a decision, that decision is going to directly or indirectly influence countless other people. Right decisions by the right people can influence people positively, so make good decisions.

———————————

You will never get ahead of others as long as you're trying to get even with them.

Ambition—Good or Bad?

*I*t is my conviction that ambition, fueled by compassion, wisdom, and integrity, is a powerful force for good. It will turn the wheels of industry and open the door of opportunity for you and countless thousands of other people. But fueled by greed and the lust for power, ambition is a destructive force that ultimately does irreparable damage to the individual in its grasp and to the people within its reach.

It is more than just a cliché to say that ambition can either make us or break us. It makes us when we hear the words of Henry Van Dyke, who said, "There is a loftier ambition than merely to stand high in the world. It is to stoop down and lift mankind a little higher." George Matthew Adams observed, "He climbs highest who helps another up." John Lubbock put it this way: "To do something, however small, to make others happier and better is the highest ambition, the most elevating hope, which can inspire a human being."

As a youngster in Yazoo City, Mississippi, I frequently heard my mother and the man for whom I worked in the grocery store describe an individual by saying, "He is really a very ambitious young man," or "She really has a lot of ambition." The tone of

> *Lack of direction, not lack of time, is the problem. We all have twenty-four-hour days.*

voice indicated that they were very favorably identifying one of the traits of that young person. I understood implicitly that they were talking about ambition fueled by compassion, wisdom, and integrity. On the other hand, I heard them say on numerous occasions, "He is a nice person, but he just doesn't have any ambition."

From my perspective, people who have ability—and that includes anyone reading these words—and do not use that ability represent one of the real tragedies of life. The old saying that you either "use it or lose it" is true. In a nutshell, ambition, fueled with compassion and direction, can be a powerful force for good.

———————

"It was so cold where we were," one man boasted, "that the candle froze and we couldn't blow it out." "That's nothing!" said the other. "Where we were the words came out of our mouths in little pieces of ice and we had to fry them to see what we were talking about." (*Courier Journal* magazine)

From Sharecropper's Daughter to College President

*M*y mother used to say, "As the twig is bent, the tree shall grow." I believe that Ruth Simmons, the new president of the highly prestigious Smith College in Massachusetts, is the classic example of the truth of that statement. She is also the epitome of the American Dream and living proof that it is still alive and well in America.

As a child, Ms. Simmons told one of her classmates that someday she would be the president of a college. That was a remarkable statement coming from the twelfth child of Texas sharecroppers. Little did she know that it would be the presidency of one of the most respected schools in the country. She is the first African-American woman to head a top-ranked college or university. Since female presidents—specifically African-American female college presidents—are rare, let's explore what happened.

Most success stories begin with the parents, and in this particular

> *All of us are shaped by what others expect of and from us. We live either up to or down to what others believe about us and what we can do. Actually, what other people think of us is frequently more crucial and influential than what we think of ourselves.*

case the emphasis is on the mother. She stressed the importance of having character and moral fiber and valuing "certain things with regard to the treatment of human beings." Ms. Simmons then said, "I worked hard at everything I did, but I didn't work hard because I was interested in good grades . . . or because I was looking for praise or enrichment, but because that is what I was taught." Ross Campbell, M.D., says that 80 percent of a child's character is formed by age five, and apparently, Ms. Simmons's character bears this out.

The selection committee at Smith emphasized that Ms. Simmons wasn't selected because she was an African-American woman. Peter Rose, a member of the search committee, said, "We wanted to cast the widest possible net for the best possible person. It was the strength of this woman. Her very strong academic performance. The force of her personality."

Let me suggest that if you raise your child with strong moral values as the Simmons family did, you, too, may be nurturing a future college president!

My mother had been complaining of dizziness, so Dad took her to the doctor's office for a checkup. She finished early, went shopping, and told Dad, "I feel much better now that I bought myself a new hat." "Good," Dad replied. "You're all dressed up and no vertigo." (Contributed to *Reader's Digest* by Betty Booher Jones)

The Power of the Word

*F*requently, we become so pragmatic that we fail to be effective. Years ago the editor of the *Dallas Morning News* pointed out to the sportswriters that "Bill" was not a suitable substitute for "William," and "Charlie" was not a suitable substitute for "Charles." Taking him literally, one of the sportswriters, in the heyday of Doak Walker of Southern Methodist University, wrote about an important game. In his story he pointed out that in the third quarter Doak Walker had left the game with a "Charles horse." I think you'll agree that the story lost some meaning with the use of "Charles."

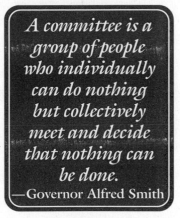

A committee is a group of people who individually can do nothing but collectively meet and decide that nothing can be done.
—Governor Alfred Smith

Perhaps the ultimate absurdity occurred in an article in a national publication when the writer set up the computer to analyze Lincoln's Gettysburg Address. Incidentally, that address contains 362 words and 302 of them are one syllable. It's simple and direct but powerful and effective.

The computer, however, made some recommendations about how the speech really should have been given. For example, instead of saying, "Four score and seven years," the computer deemed that approach too wordy and suggested, "Eighty-seven years." The efficiency in the reduction is obvious, but the loss of effectiveness, power, drama, and passion is even more obvious. When Lincoln said, "We are engaged in a great civil war," the computer questioned whether the word *great* was justified. This despite the fact that our nation suffered 646,392 casualties, including 364,511 deaths. The computer stated that the sentences were too long, and it criticized the statement that we could never forget what happened at Gettysburg as being negative. I think you'll agree that eloquence and drama, combined with passion, logic, and common sense, are far more effective in inspiring people to do great things than technical correctness.

Think about it. Knowing their power, use your words carefully. You'll be a greater contributor to humankind.

———————

Midwinter note received by the weather bureau: "Have just shoveled two feet of partly cloudy off my driveway."

Appearance Counts

*A*ccording to a recent study, the way we look has a direct bearing on a paycheck. Researchers analyzed employment data from seven thousand adults. They divided the group according to looks and then compared what those working similar jobs in each category were paid. Those who were below average in appearance earned less than those rated average. Those who rated average earned less than those who were rated above average.

Appearance includes many things. The style and neatness of your clothing, the shine on your shoes, the crease in your shirt, your choice of colors, and a host of other things affect your appearance rating. The way you fix your hair, your makeup, and all the elements of your personal grooming make a contribution. However, the biggest factor is the smile on your face, followed closely by your attitude and sense of humor. A good sense of humor and a positive attitude are particularly important as you move into the upper echelons of business.

> *Humble people don't think less of themselves; they just think of themselves less.*

The reality is that people promote people. Evidence is solid that when everything else is equal, we will promote the person we like versus the one about whom we might feel either neutral or negative almost regardless of skills. The question is, Whom do we like? I believe you'll agree that the people who are pleasant, cheerful, and optimistic are easier to like than the ones who are inclined to be dour and even negative in their approach. It's also true that the cheerful, optimistic person is going to get more done and will have more cooperation from fellow workers than will the negative individual. It's a practical matter that employers seek those who "fit," get more done, and are pleasant to be around.

So let your Sunday best appearance include a smile, a great attitude, and an easy sense of humor. Try it and I'll bet you, too, will join the ranks of the above average in salary and success in life. Take this advice to heart.

———————————

An optimist thinks the glass is half-full; a pessimist thinks the glass is half-empty. A realist knows that if he sticks around, either way he's eventually going to have to wash the glass. (*Los Angeles Times* Syndicate in *Executive Speechwriter Newsletter*)

Why Worry?

*W*orry has been described as "interest paid on trouble before it comes due." One of America's worst enemies is worry. Worry is like a rocking chair; it requires a lot of energy, and it gets you nowhere. Leo Buscaglia said, "Worry never robs tomorrow of its sorrow, it only saps today of its joy."

Question: Are you a worrier? Americans take more pills to forget more worries about more things than ever before and more than people in any other nation in history. That's bad. According to Dr. Charles Mayo, "Worry affects the circulation and the whole nervous system. I've never known a man who died from overwork, but I've known many who have died from doubt." Doubt always creates worry, and in most cases, lack of information raises the doubt.

Mathematically speaking, it really doesn't make sense to worry. Psychologists and other researchers tell us that roughly 40 percent of what we worry about will never happen and 30 percent has already happened. Addition-

Life is much like Christmas. You're more apt to get what you expect than what you want.

ally, 12 percent of our worries are over unfounded health concerns. Another 10 percent of our worries involve the daily miscellaneous fretting that accomplishes nothing. That leaves only 8 percent. Plainly speaking, Americans are worrying 92 percent of the time for no good reason, and if Dr. Mayo is right, it's killing us.

One solution that will reduce your worry is this: Don't worry about what you can't change. Example: For a number of years I've flown in excess of two hundred thousand miles a year. On occasion, flights are canceled or delayed. As I write this, I'm sitting on the runway waiting for my gate to clear. If I worry or get angry, nothing will change. If I take constructive action and finish this chapter, I'm ahead of the game. That's a positive way to use the energy that I would have wasted on anger, frustration, or worrying.

The message is clear: If you don't like your situation in life, don't fret or worry—do something about it. Worry less, and act more.

———————

To people who want to be rich and famous, I'd say . . . "Get rich first and see if that doesn't cover it." (Bill Murray)

Tying Your Shoes

*R*oger Crawford was sixteen years old before he could tie his shoes, and even then Velcro made it possible. But he excelled in other areas such as sports, becoming a star tennis player. While in high school he was a championship player, winning more than 95 percent of his matches. He continued at nearly the same pace in college and has succeeded as a pro.

You can look at Roger and see that he has a disability. As Roger explains it, however, most people's disabilities cannot be seen, but they're just as real and in many cases more pronounced than his.

Roger was born with one leg missing from the knee down. He doesn't have hands complete with four fingers and a thumb. As a matter of fact, he has only two extensions from where fingers usually are, and yet he uses the two extensions to accomplish some remarkable successes. Roger doesn't complain about what he does not have, but makes full use of what he does have. This attitude enabled him to become the first athlete with severe disabilities to compete in an NCAA division college sport.

> *Some people find fault as if there were a reward for it. Others see good in every difficulty.*

Roger doesn't pretend it's been easy, but then life is seldom easy for most of us. Today, Roger is one of the most effective public speakers in our country and a very successful published author and family man. He speaks to companies almost literally all over the world, and they range from the Fortune 500 to trade and educational associations. My suggestion to all of us is to adopt more of the Roger Crawford attitude.

Politicians like to brag that they are beefing up the economy. Obviously, they don't know beef from pork.

Leaders Accept Responsibility

*H*akeem Olajuwon is the all-pro center for the Houston Rockets, the world's champions of the National Basketball Association in 1994 and 1995. The year before they won their first championship against the New York Knicks, Hakeem realized that because he was the team leader, his responsibility was more pronounced than anyone else's. He recognized that he had a weakness in his game, which was the fifteen-foot jump shot. Think about it. He earned a multimillion-dollar income and had been all-pro for six consecutive years. However, he felt that the team would never win a championship until he improved his shooting from fifteen feet.

The real reward for a thing well done is to have done it.

Before the 1993–94 season, he went to the gym every day and practiced five hundred fifteen-foot jump shots. That's an incredible test of building strength, endurance, and improvement in performance. In 1994, when the Houston Rockets defeated the New York Knicks in seven games, there was only one game with more than a five-point difference in the score. Replays revealed that had Hakeem not improved his shooting percentage from fifteen feet, the New York Knicks would have won instead of the Houston Rockets.

Here are some questions for you to think about: First, do you believe that Hakeem is popular with his teammates as a result of the extra effort he made to help bring the championship to Houston? Second, do you believe Hakeem was thrilled to win that world's championship ring? And third, do you understand why he got a significant raise when his contract was up for renewal?

It's true, you can have everything in life you want if you will just help enough other people get what they want. Hakeem helped his teammates, the owners, and the fans gain that championship. He won big-time because he, too, was part of the championship team and, as a matter of fact, was named the most valuable player for his tremendous efforts.

If you are wearing out the seat of your pants before you do your shoe soles, you're making too many contacts in the wrong place. (Anonymous)

Prevention—The Best "Cure" for Addiction

*F*ormer drug czar William Bennett says that we can do some things to prevent our kids from ever experimenting with drugs. According to him, children who have good lines of communication with their parents, who attend church regularly and engage in extracurricular activities (sports, band, debating team, etc.), seldom try drugs. He encourages us to keep the kids busy and to remind them that they are moral and spiritual beings. He says to tell them that drug abuse is a degradation of character and the spirit, something not worthy of them.

Drug authority Dr. Forest Tennant adds a couple of significant thoughts. He says that order in a person's life is most helpful. He recommends structure and a schedule centered on positive activities. Things such as eating meals with the family, having regular times to go to bed and to get up, and setting aside a definite time to study are very helpful to young people. He also points out that you can teach kids what you know, but you will reproduce what you are. If you experiment with drugs, chances are much higher that your children will experiment with drugs and perhaps become addicts.

> *If people aren't responsible in their personal life, there is a good chance they are also irresponsible at work.*
> —Stephen F. Arterburn

Specifically, Dr. Tennant says that if your children see you drinking beer or cocktails, as far as they're concerned, you're taking something to reframe your thinking. They will view that as desirable, and the concept of drug use becomes acceptable to them. Dr. Tennant points out that tobacco and alcohol are invariably the entrance drugs to illegal drugs. This fact is reinforced in an issue of *U.S. News & World Report,* which states that there is seldom, if ever, a case of a person getting involved in illegal drugs who did not start with tobacco and/or alcohol.

William Bennett's suggestions, combined with Dr. Tennant's thoughts, are marvelous guidelines and something for every parent to consider.

Families, companies, and neighborhoods should stick together. Remember, the banana gets skinned only when it gets away from the bunch.

The Bounce-Back Kid

*H*e died three times on the way to the hospital after a head-on collision on his motorcycle caused by a car abruptly turning into his lane. I'm talking about a remarkable young man named Billy Wright, but I'm getting ahead of the story.

While in college, Billy persuaded his father to sign a note with him for $125,000 so he could buy a motorcycle dealership. After he signed the note, it occurred to him that he had no one-on-one sales experience. He went to bookstores, bought numerous books on sales and motivation, and studied them. He decided that the best way to build a business was to build repeat business, so he became heavily involved in relationship selling and did constant follow-up on all of his customers. His business the first year was $250,000, and after eight years, he was doing $1.5 million a year. Roughly 80 percent of his sales were repeat sales. Things were going well—then the accident.

Billy was unconscious for four and a half months. His injuries were so severe that his doctors

> *Your past is important, but it is not important enough to control your future.*

said that if he had been a smoker and had not been in such superb physical condition, he wouldn't have survived.

Through the four and a half months of coma, he lost seventy pounds. The first year he was awake he began what he calls the most important educational year of his life. His wife provided him with books and tapes, and for the next twelve months, Billy says he learned more than he had the previous twenty-seven years of his life. It was a turning point and prepared him for what lay ahead.

The trauma and expense were too much, and he lost almost everything, including his wife, money, and business, but he still had a positive attitude and the will to win. Today, he is busy building a successful career in the automobile business.

It's true. The person who won't be beat can't be beat. Buy that idea, and maintain the right attitude.

———————

The husband to his wife, "In the 16 years we've been married, we haven't been able to agree on a single thing." His wife replied, "It's been 17." (Executive Speechwriter Newsletter)

The Power of Attitude

*M*y friend and associate John Maxwell says, "Never underestimate the power of your attitude. It is the advance man of our true selves. Its roots are inward, but its fruit is outward. It is our best friend, or our worst enemy. It is more honest and more consistent than our words. It has an outward look based on past experiences. It is the thing which draws people to us or repels them. It is never content until it is expressed. It is the librarian of our past; it's the speaker of our present, and it's the prophet of our future."

Many people have stated that attitudes are more important than facts, and research establishes that something like 85 percent of the reason we get jobs and get ahead in those jobs has to do with our attitudes. Unfortunately, among too many of our youth today, when someone speaks of attitude, it's invariably a reference to a bad one.

Attitude is the key to education. It's the key to getting along with others and moving ahead in life. The student with a right attitude is more than willing to study to accomplish the objective of passing. A worker with the right attitude will learn to do the job

> *Do not end a meeting until a who and when to each problem have been assigned to a specific individual with an appropriate solution. A decision without a deadline is a meaningless discussion.*

better and proceed cheerfully in doing that job. The husband or wife with the right attitude will handle difficult situations in a much more effective way and enhance the relationship substantially. The physician with the right attitude will have a leg up in administering care to patients.

When everything else is equal or if there is any doubt, the coach will always choose the athlete with the best attitude. So will the employer or the man or woman seeking a mate. Message: Develop a winning attitude.

———————

When asked to clean his room, the teenager responded with feigned dismay: "What? You want me to create an imbalance in the natural ecology of my environment?" (Dorothea Kent)

Leaders Are Managers

*W*e hear a lot of discussion, read a lot of articles, and look at an amazing number of books on leadership and management. They are different functions, but leaders need to know a great deal about managing and managers need to know a lot about leading. More than 98 percent of all American companies are comprised of fewer than one hundred people. The overwhelming majority of them employ fewer than fifty. This means that the roles of leader and manager often fall on the same shoulders. Therefore, it is imperative that each knows something about leading and managing. This is also true in the family.

In the business world, the manager is in the trenches and on the front line, getting his hands dirty. He handles the daily responsibilities of dealing with his people in an effective way. He

Bring ideas in and entertain them royally, for one of them may be king.
—Martin Van Doren

makes certain that what needs to be done is done in an effective and timely manner. On the other hand, a leader encourages the manager while the manager enforces the leader's program.

The leader has an aura that frequently goes with being the head of the organization. The manager exposes his warts in his daily interchanges with his people and uses discipline when necessary. That's one of the reasons the leader must regularly support the manager and his role—so the entire team gets the full message. The leader must also understand that the way he treats the manager is the way the manager will treat his people and the way those people will treat their customers.

In an ideal situation, the leader makes the manager more effective, and the manager makes the leader more effective. The leader gives the manager responsibility as well as authority, support, and encouragement. It's safe to say that leaders, then, are the spark of encouragement that lights someone else's torch of hope who, in turn, passes it on. If you aspire to a position of leadership, implement that idea.

My teenage son is finally at peace with himself, but he still fights with everyone else. (Family Life)

Doing Beats Talking
Every Time

*C*hances are good you read the story, then probably gave it little, if any, additional thought. It was interesting, fascinating, unbelievable, and inspiring. At the time, you were probably thinking, *Maybe I should attempt a little more in my own life*.

I'm writing about the fact that Dick Rutan and Jeana Yeager in 1986 flew nonstop around the world—all 24,987 miles of it—in a specially built airplane with an unusually small engine and extremely large wings. Needless to say, there were months of preparation and many exhausting hours of anxiety as they planned the trip. There were also some extremely anxious moments when an electrical pump, designed to draw fuel from the tank, failed. Unexpected turbulence along the way bounced Jeana against the cabin wall, resulting in minor injuries, but they succeeded and even made it ahead of schedule.

Approximately fifty thousand people gathered at Edwards Air Force Base to welcome them home. For a brief time they were celebrities in the minds and hearts of millions of people, but

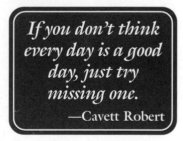

If you don't think every day is a good day, just try missing one.
—Cavett Robert

that was yesterday. Such is life itself. Incidentally, Mobil Oil Corporation provided a synthetic oil for what the company described as "the toughest test in history." Mobil then bought a full-page ad in *USA Today* to congratulate the two pilots on their record-breaking flight. The ad closed with these words: "We believed it could be done, but you, Dick and Jeana, proved it and doing beats talking every time."

Truer words were never spoken. Here are more true words. Though Dick and Jeana might be out of the public eye and the millions who applauded them for their accomplishment no longer even think about them, the major point is this: For the rest of their lives, they will remember that they did the impossible. Those memories will give them hope and encouragement to do even more. The message is clear: Take a few calculated risks in your life, and give it your best shot.

Anyone can be tenacious if he'll just hang in there long enough.

He's Eighty-Five But
Who's Counting?

*B*ob Curtis is a lively eighty-five-year-old man who married at age eighty. That in itself is remarkable, but very recently, Bob took a missionary trip to Kenya, where the pace he kept would have exhausted many people half his age. While Bob was on the six-week crusade, he spent eight days trekking the village trails outside Nairobi, the Kenyan capital, because there were no cars or streets.

To this day, Bob still works full-time on the *three* jobs he acquired to finance his trip to Kenya. He puts in three consecutive ten-hour days each week as a driver for a car auction; Saturdays are devoted to a Dallas funeral home; and he is also a regional sales representative for a dental company. With his fabulous attitude, Bob smiles and says, "Whatever it takes. If I'm able, I'll do it," and that seems to be the guiding principle of his life.

Bob knows that it's just a question of time before this life is over for him, so while he was in Nairobi he trained one of the

> *It's your attitude, not your aptitude, that determines your altitude.*

local people to continue his work. Since 1990, Bob has been on every continent and in twenty-one countries. At the moment, he is planning trips to Sweden and France. Bob credits God with his good health and ability to travel widely. His faith is such that he says he never experienced an anxious moment overseas because he believes if God challenges him, then God will enable him to do it.

With faith and an attitude like that, who knows—maybe ten years from now I'll be writing another chapter about Bob Curtis and his worldwide travels. The Bob Curtis story is certainly an inspirational example for all of us. He is a man of action. Follow Bob's example and attitude.

Saying we are in a slow recovery, not a recession, is like saying we don't have any unemployed, we just have a lot of people who are really late for work. (Comedian Jay Leno, *Executive Speechwriter Newsletter*)

Get To or Got To?

*E*very morning for several years, promptly at 10:00 A.M., a prominent businesswoman visited her mother in a nursing home. She was close to her mother and loved her very much. Often she had requests for appointments at that time of day. Her response was always the same: "No, I've got to visit with my mother." Eventually, her mother died. Shortly thereafter someone asked the woman for an appointment at 10:00 A.M. It suddenly hit her that she could no longer visit her mother. Her next thought was, *Oh, I wish I could visit my mother just one more time*. From that moment on, she changed her "got to's" to "get to's."

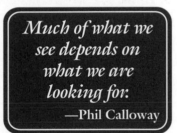

Much of what we see depends on what we are looking for.
—Phil Calloway

Her story makes us realize that pleasurable things are "get to's." I get to play golf today, or I get to go on vacation this week. Burdensome things are "got to's." I've got to go to work at 7:00 A.M. tomorrow, or I've got to clean house. Since perceptions influence thinking and performance, try this. Instead of saying, "I've got to go to work," think about people who have no job. Then you can enthusiastically change it to, "I get to go to work tomorrow." If somebody invites you to go fishing, instead of saying, "No, I've got to go to my child's game on Saturday," think about the fact that someday your child will grow up and you won't be able to go to his or her games. Then it's easy to change it to "get to."

It's amazing what that change in words will eventually do for your attitude. You'll find yourself looking forward to doing those things instead of feeling as if you *have* to do them. With a difference in attitude, there will be a difference in performance. With a difference in performance, there will be a difference in rewards. So think about these things, and change your "got to's" to "get to's."

From a book critique: "I've seen better writing on the side of a Shredded Wheat box." (Stephanie Mansfield in the *Washington Post*)

Why Not Use What Works?

*A*ccording to an August 15, 1995, column by Marvin Olasky in the *Wall Street Journal,* on July 17, about 325 people stood in the midday sun for two hours to sing "When the Saints Go Marching In" and listen to heated, socially conservative rhetoric. The demonstrators were there to defend a highly successful drug treatment program called Teen Challenge of South Texas, but the state bureaucrats stuck to their demand that the program close down or face fines of up to $4,000 a day plus jail time.

> **Bureaucracy:** *A group of disorganized, inept people totally committed to increasing their numbers in order to convert pure raw energy into solid waste.*

The bureaucrats have for thirty years told drug treatment groups that they must rely on licensed professional counselors with theoretical training rather than the ex-addicts and reformed alcoholics who lead many of the 130 chapters of Teen Challenge around the country. Sidney Watson, chairman of the local Teen Challenge Board in San Antonio, says, "I've referred people to secular counseling but that usually accomplishes only a dropping out. Our program changes lives."

Teen Challenge doesn't conform to all the paperwork, nor do all of the stairs have "uniform, nonslip surfaces," yet Teen Challenge has a long-term cure rate of 67 percent to

85 percent among program graduates. A Department of Health and Human Services Review Panel, during the 1980s, found Teen Challenge to be the best and least expensive of three hundred antiaddiction programs they examined.

Teen Challenge, which treats clients for $25 per day while fancy programs cost $600 per day and are dramatically less effective, cannot afford to have licensed counselors, so the program was to be closed down.

Dyrickey O. Johnson was in and out of state-approved expensive centers: "You had your own room . . . [and] were told to focus on your mind and your willpower . . . [but] a drug addict doesn't have any willpower." Johnson always returned to crack cocaine and alcohol until he went to Teen Challenge. He has been clean since he graduated from the program in 1992 and is now married with two small children.

I'm glad to report that San Antonio's Teen Challenge is still in the business of curing addicts and changing lives.

Message: Common sense and practical application are still the best ways to get to the top. Give both a try.

Unfortunately, you have to listen to some people for a long time to discover that they don't have anything to say.

Making the Ball Bounce
Your Way

*M*any times I use the expression, "It's not what happens to you, but how you handle what happens to you, that's going to make the difference." Initially, the ball appeared not to have bounced Celeste Baker's way, but that was just initially. She has a disease in her left leg called reflex sympathetic dystrophy, which causes her a considerable amount of pain. The way Celeste is handling her challenge is such an encouragement to her classmates at Baldwin Junior-Senior High School in Baldwin, Florida, that she was given the "I CAN" Award (a character-based achievement award) for the school year 1994–95. The next example helps explain why.

One day, Celeste called her mother to come to the school. Assuming she wanted to go home because she was in pain, Officer Keith M. Jowers, the school resource officer, in an effort to

> *People forget how quickly you completed a job, but they will remember how well you did it.*

encourage her said, "Well, at least you get to leave school early." Celeste immediately responded, "Oh, no, Officer Jowers, I just want her to bring me my crutches, so I can walk." She refused to miss the rest of school that day.

Celeste really does have a "can-do" attitude. She plays volleyball and is currently on the swim team. She even uses swim competitions as therapy. Some of the things her teachers say about her are, "She's a very creative and delightful student," and "Celeste has been a delight to teach this year," and "Celeste is a dedicated and hardworking student that [*sic*] is a joy to have in my class." Yes, in many ways she epitomizes the "I CAN" attitude. Certainly, her approach to life is a great one. As I say, it's not what happens to you, but it's how you handle it that will make the difference. Buy that idea, and adopt the "I CAN" attitude.

––––––––––

The nation's clean-air laws arose out of "the desire of people in Denver to see the mountains and the desire of people in Los Angeles to see each other." (William Ruckleshaus)

Leadership That Leads

Danny Cox's book, *Leadership When the Heat's On,* offers some exciting and very valuable tips on leadership. Here are just a few of them:

First, employees get better as their manager does, and they really don't care how smart or talented you are. What people care about is your attitude toward them.

Second, leaders have contagious enthusiasm, and as Cox points out, if you don't have that enthusiasm, please understand that whatever you do have is also contagious.

Third, when you make a list of things to do for the next day, do not go to number two as you finish the first one. Instead, under-

> *Before you can lead anyone else, you must first learn to manage yourself.*

stand that what was number two now becomes number one, and psychologically, it becomes more important when you give it a higher priority to get that job done as well. Follow that procedure through numbers two, three, and so on.

Danny Cox also lists the ten ingredients in his recipe for leadership: (1) high ethics; (2) high energy; (3) hard work; (4) enthusiasm; (5) goal-oriented; (6) courageous; (7) priority-driven; (8) nonconformist; (9) levelheaded; and (10) committed to developing employees.

In an interview with George Foreman, Danny said he noticed George's nose and decided that here was a guy who understood pain, so he asked him, "How did you stand all that pain to become the heavyweight champ?" Foreman answered, "If I see what I want real good in my mind, I don't notice any pain in getting it." Cox then points out that idea holds true for all of us.

Danny has given us some excellent advice. I believe if more of us will take it, we'll produce more leaders in this country. Listen to Danny Cox.

———

Many senior art workshop participants were trying their hand at various skills for the first time. From behind the partition separating my oil painting class from the watercolor class came these words of sweet revenge: "I think I'll send these to my grandchildren to hang on their refrigerator." (Contributed to *Reader's Digest* by Lynda Alongi)

The Choice Is Yours

You can focus on what you do have or complain about what you don't have. I want to emphasize, however, that what we focus on plays a major role in what we're able to accomplish in life. By now surely everyone knows that Heather Whitestone, the 1995 Miss America, is and has been profoundly deaf since her eighteenth month of life. However, Heather always focused on what she did have, not on what she did not have. She focused on her ability, not her disability. Heather is fortunate that she has parents who fervently believe in her and have supported, loved, encouraged, and worked with her in everything she has done.

This beautiful young woman has a keen mind. She also has tremendous spirit and a solid faith, and she has been a persistent hard worker all of her life. She is a skilled lip-reader, and

> *When you are the right kind of person, doing the right thing, help and encouragement come from all directions.*

over the years, many professors and others have helped her. Some of them have even taken the time to make copies of their notes for her.

Major point: Countless other people have also had problems, but they focused on the problems instead of the solutions to the problems. Please understand I'm making an observation and not a criticism. No one knows how other people feel, and some problems are beyond human solution.

However, my observation has been that people with a cooperative, loving, enthusiastic, gentle, positive attitude will attract people by the score who not only are willing to help them, but also are anxious to do so. The attitude about your condition, on many occasions, is even more significant than the condition itself.

Too often the opportunity knocks, but by the time you disengage the chain, push back the bolt, unhook the two locks and shut off the burglar alarms, it's too late. (Rita Cooledge)

His Commitment Was Total

*I*n the world of golf many names are legendary—Jack Nicklaus, Byron Nelson, Bobby Jones, Ben Hogan, Arnold Palmer, among others. However, considering all factors, there are many who say that Ben Hogan would have to rate at or close to the top of the totem pole.

Hogan's accomplishments are too numerous to mention, but they include 242 top ten finishes in PGA Tour events between 1932 and 1970. Hogan won 30 tournaments between 1946 and 1948, after returning from two years in the army. However, he is best remembered for the fact that on February 2, 1949, his car collided head-on with a Greyhound bus and he was nearly killed. Doctors initially doubted he would survive. Next, they predicted he would never walk or play golf again, but just sixteen months later, he was walking down the eighteenth fairway at Merion Golf Club in Ardmore, Pennsylvania, putting the finishing touches on the storybook victory at the 1950 U.S. Open.

His name is usually mentioned with awe, and people consistently make comments about the intensity of his game, his commitment to practice, his total concentration on the issue at hand, and his absolute unwillingness to settle for anything less than his best effort. He probably studied the game of golf more than anybody in history, and he

> *It's true.
> Spectacular
> preparation
> precedes
> spectacular
> performance.*

worked diligently from dawn to dusk on the practice range, perfecting every facet of his game.

I know that you may not be a golfer, but I talk about Hogan because the qualities that made him a great golfer would have made him a success in virtually any field of endeavor. He had an unbelievable commitment and a strong work ethic. He studied the game as few, if any, ever had, and he had an absolute conviction that he could improve, regardless of the state of his game. I'm persuaded that if you'll adopt these qualities and focus on your chosen job or career, you will experience success.

———————————

If you have a tendency to brag, just remember it's not the whistle that pulls the train. (O. F. Nichols)

Conviction Is the Key

*T*he late Mary Crowley frequently commented that one person with a conviction would do more than a hundred who only had an interest. Commitment is the key to staying the course and completing the project. Conviction always precedes commitment.

When you're convinced as a salesperson that you are selling a marvelous product, your demeanor, body language, voice inflection, and facial expressions communicate to the prospect that you fervently believe you're offering something of value. Many times the prospect will buy, not because of her belief in the product, goods, or service, but because of the belief of the salesperson in the product being offered.

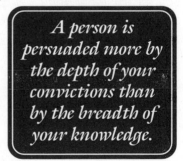

A person is persuaded more by the depth of your convictions than by the breadth of your knowledge.

Our feelings are transferable. Courage can be and frequently is transferred to the other person. Convictions are the same. The teacher who fervently believes in the message he delivers will persuade the student by the very depth of that conviction. One of my favorite Mary Kay Ash quotes is, "Many people have gone a lot farther than they thought they could because someone else thought they could." In short, their confidence, born of someone else's conviction, had enabled them to make it. Conviction comes from knowledge and a feeling that what we're teaching, doing, or selling is absolutely right. When we transfer that conviction to those within our sphere of influence, they and society benefit.

Show me a person with deep convictions and I'll show you a person who has made a commitment to deliver those convictions to others. Show me a great leader and I'll show you a person of deep convictions who is able to attract followers because of those convictions. I'll also show you a person who is happy in what she is doing and far more successful than people who do not have those convictions. Message: Buy that idea, develop those convictions, and make that commitment.

———————————

I'm certain all of us have heard about the employee who always gives his company an honest day's work. Of course, it takes him a week to do it. (Executive Speechwriter Newsletter)

Motivation, Manipulation, and Leadership

*T*he word *motivation* is often confused with *manipulation*. Motivation occurs when you persuade others to take an action in their own best interests. Things such as people preparing their homework, accepting responsibility for their performance, and finishing their education are the results of motivation. Manipulation is persuading others to take an action that is primarily for your benefit. Things such as selling an inferior product at an inflated price and working people overtime with no extra pay are examples of manipulation.

Manipulation self-destructs the individual doing the manipulating. Word gets out on manipulators, and people grow less and less likely to respond in a positive manner to their manipulation. Productivity declines. Leadership occurs when you persuade a person to take an action that is in your mutual best interests. Dwight Eisenhower said that leadership was the ability to persuade someone to do what you wanted him to do because he wanted to do it. When that happens, performance improves, productivity increases, and both parties win.

Comparing motivation to manipulation is like comparing kindness to deceit. The difference

> *A fair-weather friend is always there when he needs you.*

is the intent of the person. Motivation will cause people to act out of free choice and desire, while manipulation often results in forced compliance. One is ethical and long-lasting; the other is unethical and temporary.

Thomas Carlisle said, "A great man shows his greatness by the way he treats the little man." The value you place on people determines whether you are a motivator or a manipulator of people. Motivation is moving together for mutual advantage. Manipulation is persuading or even subtly coercing people to do something so that you win and they lose. With the motivator, everybody wins; with the manipulator, only the manipulator wins. And to that I might add that the victory is temporary and the price is prohibitive.

Leaders and motivators are winners; manipulators are losers who produce resentment and discord. Become a motivator, lead your people, and don't manipulate them.

Overheard: "I spend a lot of money . . . but name me one other extravagance!"

It's in the Heart

*I*n today's world the typical college basketball player is so tall, he can look a giraffe eyeball-to-eyeball. For that reason, the fact that Keith Braswell, standing just four feet eleven and one-half inches tall, made the Dayton University basketball team is little short of unbelievable. He is the shortest player in the school's history by two and a half inches. This Flyers freshman looks up to Muggsy Bogues who is all of five feet three and plays in the NBA for the Charlotte Hornets. He is considerably shorter than Spud Webb, who was the first truly short player to make the NBA.

Perhaps the most remarkable thing is that he made the team as a walk-on. He is incredibly quick, has a great three-point shot, is an excellent ball handler, and is even pretty good at rebounding. Part of his success is summed up by a competitive coach, Mike Calhoun from Eastern Kentucky, who says that "Keith has a big heart," and "his passion and enthusiasm excite the crowd." Keith Braswell gives both men and women of short stature—and for that matter, people who have perceived or real disadvantages or disabilities—the all-important ingredient called "hope."

> *It's not just the size of the dog in the fight; it's the size of the fight in the dog.*

All of this is to say that it's relatively easy to put people on a pair of scales and tell exactly how much they weigh. You can stand them up and measure their exact height. But it is impossible to measure the human qualities that coaches constantly refer to as "heart." When we recognize, use, and develop what is inside us to the fullest capacity, it's amazing what we can do with our lives. Keep your eyes on this young man; he is a hope builder.

"Can you tell me where I will find the book Man, the Superior Sex?*" the man asked the saleswoman. "Sure, it's upstairs in the science fiction department," she replied.*

Miss Amy Whittington Is a Difference Maker

*I*n our lifetime, each one of us influences both by word and by deed—either for good or for bad—countless numbers of people. That means all of us are difference makers.

Miss Amy Whittington would certainly qualify as one who directly and indirectly influenced thousands of people. At age eighty-three, she was still teaching a Sunday school class in Sault Sainte Marie, Michigan. She learned that the Moody Bible Institute in Chicago was offering a seminar to teach people how to be more effective teachers. She literally saved her pennies until she had the necessary money to buy a bus ticket to Chicago. She rode the bus all night to attend the seminar to learn new methods and procedures so she could do a better job.

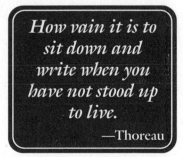

How vain it is to sit down and write when you have not stood up to live.

—Thoreau

One of the professors, impressed with her age, enthusiasm, and the fact that she had ridden the bus all night to attend the seminar, engaged her in conversation. He asked her what age-group she taught and how many were in her class. When she responded that she taught a class of junior high school boys and there were thirteen in the class, the professor asked how many kids belonged to the church. Miss Whittington replied, "Fifty." The professor, astonished that she taught more than

25 percent of the church youth, responded, "With that kind of record we should have you teach us how to teach." How right he was!

I hasten to add that people who are already good at what they do are far more likely to work at getting better than are those who are marginal performers. What kind of impact did Miss Amy Whittington have? Eighty-six of those boys she taught in her Sunday school class through the years ended up in the ministry. Can't you just imagine the thousands of people she directly and indirectly affected for good? She truly was a difference maker. You are, too, so make it a good difference.

When a man gets too big for his britches, he will find somebody else in his shoes.

The Dignity of Simplicity

*A*uthor John Maxwell writes, "There is great dignity in simplicity. Most of the immortal works of literature not only have the brilliance of brevity, but also the dignity of simplicity. The Lord's Prayer consists of only 57 words, none more than two syllables. The Declaration of Independence, which revolutionized the thinking of the entire world, can be read by a fourth-grader in less than five minutes. Simplicity is eloquent; it speaks loud and clear without insulting the intelligence of the listener."

As I read those words, I was moved to look up the word *dignity* in my trusty 1828 Noah Webster dictionary. Here is what Webster wrote: "True honor. Nobleness or elevation of mind. Consisting in a high sense of propriety, truth and justice, with an abhorrence of mean and sinful actions. It's elevation; honorable place or rank of elevation; degree of excellence, either in estimation or in the order of nature."

A parent or teacher who treats a child with dignity builds the self-esteem of the child and automatically increases the child's performance, which generally improves the child's conduct. An employer who treats employees with respect and dignity builds loyalty and increases productivity. You treat another person, regardless of age, with dignity when you courteously listen to him or her and respond in a thoughtful manner. You

> *You can't hold a man down without staying down with him.*
> —Booker T. Washington

treat others with dignity when you show them respect, regardless of their occupation, sex, race, creed, or color. And when you treat others with respect and dignity, your own self-respect and sense of dignity improve.

Simplicity and dignity make a powerful combination. When you strive for dignity and use simplicity as a yardstick, you've just elevated your possibilities for accomplishment.

Master of ceremonies addressing the audience: "And now it is my pleasure to offer the customary exaggerations of the accomplishments of our guest speaker."

The Little Town That Could

Most people, when they think of a burgeoning industrial giant, do not think of Tupelo, Mississippi. But they should! Tupelo has enthusiasm, community spirit, common sense, hard work, and commitment to moving forward in this competitive era. These qualities led economist Sheila Tschinkel to comment, "Tupelo is what we always come back to in economic development." Charles Gordon, director of corporate communications with Norbord Industries, a Canadian wood products maker, said they chose Tupelo over other competitors. They did so because "they were the most professional people we had ever encountered in industrial development circles."

The citizens' attitude and hard work have led eighteen Fortune 500 companies to set up production in this Mississippi town. The list includes such luminaries as the Sara Lee Corporation and Cooper Tire and Rubber Company and a number of furniture makers and investors from as far away as Switzerland, Brazil, and Australia.

According to a *Wall Street Journal* article, there are a number of reasons for Tupelo's success.

> *Don't ever criticize anything in your company until you've got a better way of doing it worked out on paper and you're willing to risk your reputation as an executive on its workability.*
>
> —Maxey Jarmon

First, Tupelo has a long-term commitment to investment in the community. Second, Tupelo spends heavily to build a skilled workforce and acts quickly to address minority grievances. Third, the city has people who are willing to take calculated risks. For example, George McLean, publisher of the town's *Daily Journal* from 1934 until his death in 1983, made sure things happened in Tupelo. When a shortage of factory and warehouse space threatened to stop growth in the late '50s, he mortgaged his newspaper to build more than 650,000 square feet of industrial space. This kind of attitude and commitment has attracted investors from around the world.

Combining all these factors explains why this small Mississippi town is making such great strides. As further proof, in 1991, a $17 million bond issue for a new high school passed with 89 percent voter approval. The message here is that other cities in similar circumstances can take the Tupelo approach and dramatically improve the lives of their residents.

One of the challenges facing teachers and parents is how to explain the importance of proper nutrition to kids who have grown well over six feet tall on a diet of junk food.

Respond—Don't React

Most people would agree that the loss of both arms for a three-year-old would be a tragedy beyond belief. That's what happened to Jon Paul Blenke. He and his parents quickly accepted the fact that he would be without his arms for the rest of his life and decided to adapt and use what was left and not moan about what was lost.

Unfortunately, when most people lose part of a physical or financial asset, they take the "I've lost it all and there's nothing I can do" approach. Jon Paul instinctively knew better, his parents encouraged him, and the results speak for themselves. Any parent would be proud to have Jon Paul as a son, and any coach would be delighted to have him on his team. Today, Jon Paul is an outgoing, enthusiastic, highly motivated youngster who has an incredible attitude. When someone tells him what he can't do, he starts figuring out a way to do it. He plays soccer, writes with his feet, drives the lawn mower with his legs, swims, skates, skis, and plays football.

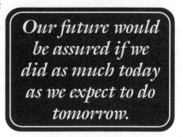

Our future would be assured if we did as much today as we expect to do tomorrow.

Coach Bob Thompson of the Leduc Bobcats says that Jon Paul is a capable player, and his teammates say "he really hits like heck." His teammates have respect for him, and the coach says he is a super athlete. "In his mind, he doesn't have a disability. The only position he won't play is quarterback, but if there's a way, he'll find it." There are few hurdles in his mind he can't overcome. If there's frustration, it's short-lived, and very seldom will he give up.

I have an idea this young man is going to do well in his life, and he already serves as a marvelous role model. I encourage you to learn from this enthusiastic youngster.

———————

"Peanuts" characters Charlie Brown and Lucy were playing marbles, and Lucy was winning. As she knocked Charlie's agates and steelies, he kept saying, "Luck, luck, luck." The second frame of the cartoon strip showed more of the same. In the third frame, Lucy was going saucily down the street with all of Charlie's marbles and he was still saying, "Luck, luck, luck." But when Lucy got around the corner, he said, "Boy, that girl can really play marbles!" (Executive Speechwriter Newsletter)

Truth Is Stranger and More Exciting Than Fiction

Gone with the Wind is the classic. *Scarlett* is the follow-up to the classic. However, the original story had more than just a kernel of truth in it. There was a Rhett Butler, but his real name was Rhett Turnipseed. Scarlett O'Hara was Emelyn Louise Hannon. Yes, Rhett did walk out on her and join the Confederate army. When the war was over, Rhett Turnipseed became a drifter and gambler. He ended up in Nashville where his life was turned around on Easter morning in 1871 when he attended a Methodist revival meeting and became a committed Christian.

Soon after, Rhett enrolled at Vanderbilt University and became a Methodist preacher. Reverend Rhett was worried about a young woman in his flock who had run away and was working in a house of prostitution in St. Louis. Rhett rode off to look for her and found her. Incredibly enough, the madam was his former love, Emelyn Louise Hannon—or Scarlett. She refused to let Rhett see the young woman, so Rhett challenged her to a game of cards. If he won, the young girl would be free; if Scarlett won, she would remain. Rhett won.

Good news—you can change; make sure it's for the better.

Fortunately, the story ends well for everyone. The young girl married well and became the matriarch of a leading family in the state. Later, Emelyn, so impressed with the change in Rhett's life, also became a Christian and joined the Methodist church. Eventually, she opened an orphanage for Cherokee children. She died in 1903. Her grave is marked to this day.

The message is twofold. First, truth really is stranger than fiction, and second, yes, people can change. Going from gambler to preacher and from madam to operator of an orphanage for displaced children represents quite a change. So don't give up. You can change.

Comic J. Scott Homan said he's been trying to get into shape doing twenty sit-ups each morning. That may not sound like a lot, but you can only hit the snooze alarm so many times.

Intelligent Selfishness

Fortune magazine published an intriguing article on a multi-billionaire from Hong Kong named Li Ka-Shing. His two sons, Victor and Richard, were raised in their father's business, attending board meetings and conferences where they were instructed, informed, and indoctrinated in their father's philosophy.

Obviously, if you're worth a few billion dollars, you have a different approach to your children from the one most of us would take. For example, how do you explain to a nine-year-old that he can't have a bicycle that costs $250 because it's too expensive when that nine-year-old has already observed that money is not a concern within the household? But Li Ka-Shing recognized that affording it was not the issue; teaching sound principles was the idea involved. For that reason, he kept a reasonably close rein on indulgences for his sons. Traditionally, youngsters growing up in extraordinarily wealthy families, not newly rich athletes or movie stars but those whose fortunes have been in the family for several generations, are familiar with financial restraint.

Perhaps the most intriguing thing Richard observed as he watched his father, who was truly

> *A person is no greater than his or her dreams, ideals, hopes, and plans. A person dreams the dream and dreams of fulfilling it. It's the dream that makes the person.*

an entrepreneurial genius, was that his dad engaged in many joint ventures with people who had products and ideas but were short on capital. Richard learned that if 10 percent is a fair percentage of the business you receive as a result of your investment, but you know you can get 11 percent, it is wise to take only 9 percent. Li Ka-Shing taught his boys that if he took less than he could get, countless other people with good ideas and good products but no money would flock to his doorstep. The net result is that instead of making one profitable—albeit greedy—deal, he could make numerous good, solid deals at the lower percentage, and the total amount of profits would be dramatically higher. That's being intelligently selfish, which is really being unselfish and wise.

A hypocrite has been accurately described as one who is not himself on Sunday.

"... To Keep Myself ..."

*T*he Scout Oath in its entirety says, "On my honor I will do my best to do my duty to God and my country and to obey the Scout Law; to help other people at all times; to keep myself physically strong, mentally awake, and morally straight."

Let's look at the final portion of that Oath: "physically strong." When we take care of our bodies, we're energized to do more in our personal, family, and business lives. One study of top-level executives revealed that 93 percent of them have a high energy level. Less than 10 percent of them smoke, 90 percent of them exercise regularly, and virtually all of them know their cholesterol levels. The benefits of physical fitness are great.

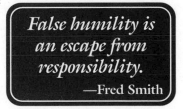

False humility is an escape from responsibility.
—Fred Smith

Being "mentally awake" is obviously important in our day of change at a pace unheard of in history. Mental preparation through reading, attending seminars, listening to or viewing educational audio- and videotapes, and studying are certainly part of a youngster's life. In addition, the things they learn in Scouting about being mentally alert include the shunning of tobacco, alcohol, and illegal drugs, which are mind and body destroyers.

The "morally straight" portion is perhaps the most significant. One study of the CEOs of the Fortune 500 companies revealed that their number one asset was their integrity.

Members of the Harvard Business School graduating class of 1949, which is recognized as being the most outstanding class in the school's history, almost unanimously stated that their ethics, values, and commitment to being morally sound with their families were prime reasons for their success.

Putting all of these things together validates that the Scout Oath, followed in its entirety, will produce a disproportionate share of the winners in society. Think about it. Make the Scout Oath part of your life.

A man was praying, "Lord, is it true that to You a minute is like a thousand years and a penny is like a thousand dollars?" The Lord answered, "Yes." Then the man asked, "Then can I have a penny?" The Lord replied, "In a minute."

It's Never Too Late!

*I*n May of 1983, Helen Hill, age ninety-five, received her high school diploma. She was absolutely ecstatic. When she finished high school seventy-six years earlier, she and her five classmates did not receive formal diplomas because the school was so much in debt, it could not afford them. Mrs. Hill was the only surviving member of the class of 1907, so she could not share her joy and excitement with her former classmates. The message is clear: A disappointment of yesterday can turn into a delight for today. It's never too late!

Carl Carson, at the tender age of sixty-four, decided to make a career change. At that age, most people think in terms of retirement, which is unfortunate. Many sixty-four-year-olds are still very young and have accumulated experiences on which they can build exciting and rewarding careers. Carson had been successful as a car and truck leasing agent. For his new career, he decided to go into the consulting business. His original plan was to sell his services to ten clients. Like many of us, when he reached his rather modest goal, he decided to do more. He began putting out a monthly newspaper, advising

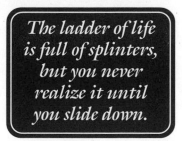

The ladder of life is full of splinters, but you never realize it until you slide down.

twelve hundred paying subscribers. By age seventy-five, Carson was crisscrossing the nation a hundred times a year, speaking at conventions and having a very good time.

The message is absolutely clear: It's never too late to dream, to learn, or to change. Too many people come up with excuses for not reaching their goals. They don't live in the right place, are too old or too young, or have a host of other excuses. I'm not saying that it's going to be easy because life is tough, but it can be rewarding! It's true that you can't stop the calendar or turn back the clock, but you can still dream, set positive goals, and use your unique abilities.

Show me a man who walks with his head held high and I'll show you man who hasn't quite gotten used to his bifocals.
(*Stripped Gears*)

Out of the Ashes

*M*any times disasters and/or tragedies spawn incredible accomplishments and enormous progress. A tornado in August of 1883 devastated Rochester, Minnesota, and yet from those ashes came the world-famous Mayo Clinic. According to Daniel J. Murphy in a recent article in *Investors Daily,* "Mother Alfred Moes, the founder of the Sisters of St. Francis, brought her untrained nuns to assist in nursing those who had been injured in the tornado. While there, she convinced the leading town doctor to head an unbuilt hospital she would raise funds to construct. That physician and surgeon's name was William Worral Mayo and the hospital, St. Mary's, was forerunner to and still affiliated with the world-famous Mayo Clinic."

In the early part of this century, the boll weevil devastated southern cotton crops, hitting particularly hard in southern Alabama. The disaster was a wake-up call for the need to diversify. The farmers of that area started raising peanuts, soybeans, corn, sorghum, fresh vegetables, and more. The economy improved so much that the residents of Enterprise, Alabama, actually built a monument to the boll weevil in the center of town.

> *Problems produce patience; patience produces persistence; persistence produces character; character produces hope; hope produces power.*

In my life a seeming disaster was a blessing in disguise. I was quickly approaching the publication date for my first book, *See You at the Top,* when my gallbladder ruptured. Because I was unable to travel, my heavy speaking schedule came to an abrupt halt for twenty-two days. During nineteen of those twenty-two days, I was able to work ten to twelve hours a day while lying in bed or sitting quietly in a chair. Had I not had those hours, the book definitely would not have met the deadline.

Message: When disaster strikes, ask, What good can come of it? In many cases, you'll discover that a temporary disaster can turn into long-term gain.

God made man. Then He stepped back, looked him over, and said, "I can do better than that," and He made woman.
(Mary Crowley)

Employability

*H*ow many of the unemployed are employable? Probably most of them—at least to a degree. But many are unemployable in the better jobs because they do not have the training, background, education, or desire to have the better jobs. It's true they would like to have someone just give them the jobs, whether they're qualified or not. However, in business and industry, workers must bring in more than they cost in wages and benefits, or the company ultimately goes bankrupt and then no one has a job.

The Lincoln Electric Company in Euclid, Ohio, had two hundred jobs available, but the company could not fill all of those jobs out of some twenty thousand applicants. The reason: They could not do high school math. So, who is at fault? Some may say the parents did not discipline them and require them to study; others may say the educational system is no longer functional in meeting needs; still others may say the government has not subsidized the education of these people enough.

Reality says that ultimately each one of us must accept responsibility to acquire the information we need to get the jobs we want. For example, for the nearly twenty thousand who could not qualify for one of those well-paying jobs at Lincoln Electric, the solution is to go directly to one of the

> *You can finish school and even make it easy. However, you will never finish your education and it is seldom easy.*

community colleges and catch up on math. Literacy Volunteers of America and/or the National Institute for Literacy would be helpful, and each applicant probably has at least one friend who is qualified and willing to help. It's true this move requires initiative and facing some embarrassment, but refusing to deal with the issue is not going to make it any easier or better.

Message: If you would like to get a better job, get help. It's amazing what three hours a week for about ten weeks will do to improve your skills, confidence, and self-esteem. Do it now—get that help, and your life will improve.

―――――――――

No wonder I had an inferiority complex as a child! My best friend was captain of the football team, star pitcher on the baseball team, high scorer on the basketball team, valedictorian of the class, and played Joseph in the Christmas play.

Work—Who Needs It?

Somebody once said that work is the father of success and integrity is the mother. If you can get along with these two members of the family, the rest of the family will be easy to deal with. However, too many people don't make enough effort to get along with the father and leave the mother out completely. Some even quit looking for work as soon as they find a job.

Many people's concept of work is that it should be fun and meaningful, or we shouldn't be expected to do it. I'm convinced that the sheer love of work, with all its rewards, should provide enormous satisfaction. Charles Gow contends that work gives you an appetite for your meals; it lends solidity to your slumber; it gives you a perfect appreciation of a holiday. The truth is, we all need work.

> *To change your friends, family, and lifestyle, you must first change yourself.*

Personally, I don't believe anyone enjoys what he does any more than I enjoy what I do, and yet certain phases of my work are tedious: constant deadlines and occasional canceled or delayed flights when I must sit in an airport or on a runway for hours, for example. These things aren't fun and meaningful, but they are part of the package of what I do, so I respond when flights are delayed and use the time for research and writing.

Voltaire said that work keeps us from three great evils: boredom, vice, and poverty. With that concept in mind we can look at the benefits and understand that "you don't 'pay the price'—you enjoy the benefits." Thomas Edison said, "There is no substitute for hard work. Genius is one percent inspiration and ninety-nine percent perspiration." Benjamin Franklin put it this way: "The used key is always bright." And finally, Richard Cumberland observed, "It is better to wear out than to rust out."

Bottom line: Unless you work, you will miss out on many of the joys and benefits of life itself. So concentrate on the things you like about your job and its benefits. Give your job that extra burst of energy you always have on the day before vacation. Not only will you enjoy your work more, but also *raise* and *praise* will both come your way.

———————

Don't overdo this work thing. Remember that the man who is always busy as a bee might awaken to discover that someone has swiped his honey.

The Entrepreneur Is Alive and Well

*S*ometimes a big loss can be the catalyst for an even bigger gain. In the early 1980s, farmers in Delta and Montrose Counties, Colorado, lost a big barley-growing contract, which put their future in question. The farming industry had suffered numerous reverses. Inflation, high interest rates, and other factors had substantially reduced the number of farms. The situation was serious, so the governor sent his economic team to preach value-added agriculture. John Harold, a local farmer and well-known figure, decided to take a gamble and bet on Olathe sweet corn. It's truly a case of taking the proverbial lemon and making lemonade. In 1985, they shipped 12,568 boxes of corn. Now they ship 500,000 cases a year. How did it happen?

> *Every problem carries the seed of an equivalent or greater benefit.*

Olathe sweet corn had long been a favorite in the Western Slope area of the country. By improving the storage and shipping process and assuring fresh delivery, Harold made it a favorite from Atlanta to Los Angeles.

Harold's role is primarily that of a coordinator as he works with twenty-five growers, including himself. They time the harvest so that it occurs over an eight-week period. The corn is boxed in the field, forty-eight ears per container. Then it's brought to Harold's 20,000-square-foot cooler by truck. A forklift removes the boxes and a machine called a clamshell injects a slush-ice mixture into each box to make certain the corn is packed cold. Seventy-five percent of the corn is on trucks headed out the day it's picked, and no corn sits in his cooler longer than three days.

By adding value to their product, the Delta and Montrose Counties farmers have opened a huge new market, a market facilitated largely by John Harold's willingness to take a risk and try something new.

If you have an entrepreneurial spirit and are willing to take some risks, you can turn lemons into lemonade.

———————

Sometimes Dad does win. The college boy wrote his father, "I can't understand how you can call yourself a kind parent when you haven't sent me a check in two months! What kind of kindness is that?" The father replied, "Son, that's called 'unremitting' kindness."

Leaders Are Communicators

*A*n old saying maintains, "That which can be misunderstood will be misunderstood." This resolution, passed by the board of councilmen in Canton, Mississippi, in the mid-1800s, focuses on an example that could be neither understood nor implemented: "Number one: Resolved by this Council that we build a new jail. Number two: Resolved that the new jail be built out of the materials of the old jail. Resolved that the old jail be used until the new jail is finished."

In many ways, effective communication begins with mutual respect—communication that inspires, encourages, or instructs others to do their best. When you respect people, you will never be rude to them. Consequently, by treating them with respect, you get cooperation, enthusiastically given instead of grudgingly given. Respected individuals are going to work harder to become peak performers, wanting to do more and more.

If people like you, they will work harder for you. If they don't like you, they might work to keep their jobs, but they won't really be giving the effort they're capa-

> *Tact is the art of building a fire under people without making their blood boil.*

ble of giving. People might perform to keep their jobs because duty and responsibility demand that they do a job well. But love and encouragement enable people to do work beautifully. When you communicate to people that you genuinely like and respect them, and follow that up with consistency of action, you establish rapport with and confidence in your people that will make a difference.

Communication is not necessarily an easy skill to learn, but it really begins with seriously listening to what the other person says. By listening with respect, you will learn things that can make a difference. Consistency will be the result, and consistent performance is the key to excellence. Buy into and practice these concepts.

———————

My boss is a man of his word and that word is cheap.

Moving Up in Life

Someone accurately stated that when you hire others smarter than yourself, you prove you are smarter than they are. We can apply that to all areas of ability. The sales manager should strive diligently to hire salespeople who are better at selling than he or she is. That way they can share information, and they will all be even more effective. Also, by continuing to learn from each salesperson, the manager will stay one step ahead of all of them. Exactly the same thing applies in coaching. A good head coach seeks assistant coaches who know more about their specialty than he does and he learns from them. Ditto for managers in manufacturing, engineering, architecture, and other fields.

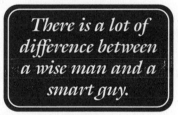

There is a lot of difference between a wise man and a smart guy.

Many years ago Lawrence Welk hired an accordionist named Myron Floren. He was considered the best in his profession. When Mr. Welk told his business manager what he had done, his business manager was furious. He felt one accordion in the orchestra was enough. Mr. Welk just smiled and said the hiring was firm. The first night the business manager heard Myron play in the orchestra with Lawrence Welk, he told Mr. Welk that the new accordion player was better than he was. Lawrence Welk smiled and confided, "That's the only kind of musician I hire." That's the best way to become a success. That also helps explain one of the reasons Mr. Welk and his "Champagne Music" spanned four generations of music lovers. Excellence and the commitment to bring customers the best possible product are the predictors of long-term success.

All of us can learn and benefit from the knowledge and talent of others. Don't be intimidated by someone with a more successful résumé, and don't feel superior to someone who has enjoyed less success than you have. Learn from both of them.

The boss read the notes in the Suggestion Box and complained that he wished the employees had been more specific. "What kind of kite? Which lake?" (*American Legion* magazine)

How to Finish Well

A few years ago my wife and I attended the musical *Crazy for You*. During the delightful performance, I observed many important principles that anyone seeking a happy and successful life should apply. First, all twenty-eight members of the cast gave their total effort from "hello" to "good-bye." Second, the enthusiasm of every performer was conspicuous. Third, regardless of the size of the part, each one gave 100 percent. Fourth, their commitment to do their best was obvious and inspiring. Fifth, through their body language and smiles, they encouraged one another. Sixth, their team spirit, including the stagehands' efforts during scenery changes, was absolutely phenomenal. Seventh, the confidence and trust they had for and in one another were wonderful. Example: Some performers fell backward off the platform, without looking, into the waiting arms of their fellow performers. Eighth, their timing was absolutely magnificent. Ninth, they had fun performing. Tenth, their preparation was obvious. Eleventh, their enthusiasm in performing increased our enjoyment in watching them.

> *Total effort, fully expended, in quest of a worthy ideal is the key to maximum performance.*

To paraphrase Will Rogers, the performers knew what they were doing, believed in what they were doing, and loved what they were doing. To take it one step farther, I would even say they had a passion for what they were doing—and it showed.

The elements that made the show successful are the same elements that can make life successful. In concert, they amount to competence and professionalism. If we add these elements to our daily lives, our productivity will increase dramatically, our future will be infinitely brighter, employment security will be substantially improved, and we will finish well. I urge you to take these steps because they are the steps up the ladder to a balanced success.

The young lawyer told his associate, "I feel like telling that judge where to get off again." "What do you mean, 'again'?" "Well," the young lawyer replied, "I felt like it last week too."

Help Others—Help Yourself

*S*omebody once made the observation that the person who is wrapped up entirely in himself makes a very small package—and the package contains an unhappy person. Think about this: Have you ever known a genuinely happy, self-centered person?

I love the story, often told, about a man who was hiking in the mountains. He was taken by surprise in a sudden snowstorm and quickly lost his way. He knew he needed to find shelter fast, or he would freeze to death. Despite all of his efforts, his hands and feet quickly went numb. In his wandering he literally tripped over another man who was almost frozen. The hiker had to make a decision: Should he help the man, or should he continue in hopes of saving himself?

In an instant he made a decision and threw off his wet gloves. He knelt beside the man and began massaging his arms and legs. After the hiker had worked for a few minutes, the man began to respond and was soon able to get on his feet. Together the two men, supporting each other, found help. The hiker was later informed that by helping another, he had helped himself. His numbness vanished while he was massaging the stranger's arms and legs. His heightened activity had enhanced his circulation and brought warmth to his hands and feet.

> *Christ said, "He who would become the greatest among you must become the servant of all."*

It's ironic but not surprising that when he lost sight of himself and his predicament and focused on someone else, he solved his own problem. It's my conviction that the only way to reach the mountain peaks of life is to forget about self and help other people reach greater heights.

———————

Strange how percentages work out. We've met two hundred people who have had their fenders smashed in parking lots, but never one that's smashed anybody else's. (Bill Vaughn)

Friends

John Cherten Collins declared, "In prosperity, our friends know us. In adversity, we know our friends." The 1828 Noah Webster dictionary says that a *friend* is "one who is attached to another by affection; one who entertains for another sentiments of esteem, respect and affection, which lead him to desire his company and to seek to promote his happiness and prosperity." In other words, it means someone who is interested in doing something for another person. A friend is an attendant, a companion, a favorer; one who is propitious. It is a term of salutation.

I agree with the statement that if, at the end of life, we can count at least two people who are true friends willing to do anything for us at the drop of a hat, who stand ready when we are hurting or need help, we are indeed fortunate. We can talk with friends about every facet of life—our joys, trials, triumphs, tragedies, hopes, wants, and needs. We can make ourselves vulnerable to them, knowing they will always think and act in our best interests. Joseph Addison held that "friendship improves happiness and abates misery by doubling our joy and dividing our grief." Robert Hall claimed, "He who has made the acquisition of a judicious and sympathizing friend may be said to have doubled his mental resources."

> *No one has so many friends he or she can afford to squander even one.*

Since friends and friendships are so valuable, how can you acquire more? If you go out in life looking for friends, they will be hard to find. If you go out in life striving to be a friend, you will find them everywhere. Samuel Johnson said, "If a man does not make new acquaintances as he advances through life, he will soon find himself left alone. A man should keep his friendship in a constant repair." Follow that advice, and you will seldom be lonely.

Illinois state representative Ellis Levin mailed a fund-raising letter that claimed he had won "special recognition" from Chicago Magazine. *Indeed he had. The magazine called him one of the state's "Ten Worst Legislators."*

She Drew the Line

You've probably never heard of Dr. June McCarroll, but she is truly one of the women who left a mark on the world. Born in Nebraska, she was a general practitioner who lived in California. Interestingly enough, her claim to fame lies outside the world of medicine. An accident was the trigger that got her thinking about making our highways safer. Her car was sideswiped, and she determined to do something about cars that crowded others off the road.

As she was driving along a road that bulged down its center, she noticed that the bulge helped to keep motorists on their own side of the road. That gave her an idea, and she started trying to persuade the town council to "paint a line down the middle of the road" to set an example and "lead the nation in public safety." She got the typical bureaucratic response that her idea was ingenious but impractical. However, Dr. McCarroll was one of those people who would not take no for an answer, so she took her idea to the local women's club. The vote was unanimous in support of the project. Nevertheless, as the saying goes, some minds are like concrete—all mixed up and permanently set. She continued to face bureaucratic stubbornness for seven long years before her idea was implemented.

C. N. Hamilton was a staunch local supporter of Dr. McCarroll's concept, and when he became a

> *If you believe—
> really believe—
> you will persist.*

member of the California Highway Commission in 1924, he

convinced the commission to approve the painting of a five-mile-long experimental center line on Route 99. An additional test strip was also painted. Accidents on both stretches diminished dramatically, and soon the entire state boasted McCarroll lines on its highways. Most of the world has since followed suit.

Message: When you conceive an idea in which you fervently believe, go after that idea, especially if people you respect believe it's a good one. Hang in there because polite, pleasant persistence is often the key to accomplishment.

———————

An optimist is someone who believes that a house fly is looking for a way to get out. (George Gene Nathan)

Love Says No to the Moment

*H*annah Moore wrote, "Love never reasons, but profusely gives—gives like a thoughtless prodigal its all, and trembles then, lest it has done too little." Dr. James Dobson wisely and accurately observes that love, in the absence of instruction, will not produce a child with self-discipline, self-control, and respect for fellow human beings. The result is a misfit.

To believe that love alone is all that's needed is a tragic misconception about real love. Love is not always giving others what they want; love is doing for others what is best for them. That reminds me of my close friend—really, he's more like a brother—Bernie Lofchick, from Winnipeg, Canada. His son, David, was born with cerebral palsy and initially had a very difficult time.

When David was about eighteen months old, Bernie and his wife, Elaine, had to put braces on David's legs every night. The doctor instructed them to make the braces progressively tighter, which caused considerable pain. Many times David pleaded, "Do we have to put them on tonight?" or "Do you have to make them so tight?" But Bernie and Elaine Lofchick loved David so much, they were able to say no to the tears of the moment so they could say yes to the laughter of a lifetime.

> *For God so loved the world that He gave His only begotten Son, that whoever believes in Him should not perish but have everlasting life.*
>
> —John 3:16 NKJV

Today, David is an active, healthy, successful businessman with a wife and three beautiful children. David's success story is the result of a love so deep that the Lofchicks were willing to do for David what was best for him—and not what David wanted at the moment.

Think about it. Make that kind of love paramount in your life.

———————

Some people are like blotters—they soak it all in but get it all backward.

Getting Even

*O*ne of these days I'm going to get even with you!" is a statement all of us are familiar with. People are either threatening to or actually getting even with others. The problem with getting even is that we will never get ahead, which most of us want to do.

I love the story of what happened during the days of the Berlin Wall. One day some of the East Berliners decided they were going to send their West Berlin adversaries a little "gift." They loaded a dump truck with garbage, broken bricks, stones, building material, and anything else with zero value. They drove the truck across the border, gained clearance, and dumped it on the West Berlin side.

Needless to say, the West Berliners were incensed and were going to "get even" with them. They were going to "pay them

> *Among the things you can give and still keep are your word, a smile, and a grateful heart.*

back." Fortunately, a very wise man intervened and gave entirely different counsel. As a result, they responded and loaded a dump truck with food (which was scarce in East Berlin), clothing (which was also scarce), medical supplies (which were even scarcer), and a host of other essential items. They took the truck across the border, carefully unloaded it all, and left a neat sign that read, "Each gives according to his ability to give."

The West Berliners had taken Booker T. Washington's

philosophy literally: "I will permit no man to narrow and degrade my soul by making me hate him." The Bible says that when you repay evil with good, you "heap coals of fire" on the other person's head. In biblical times, heaping coals of fire on an enemy's head was an act that the Lord rewarded. It makes you smile as you wonder how the East Berliners felt, along with the gratitude for the much-needed supplies. I'm willing to wager that they were somewhat embarrassed at their own attitudes.

Message: Kill 'em with kindness. Don't return evil in like kind. Be more magnanimous than that.

My six-year-old son just got a dog, so we're sending him to obedience school and if it works out, we'll send the dog, too. (*Family Life*)

This Is a Philosophy, Not a Tactic

I frequently say, "You can have everything in life you want if you will just help enough other people get what they want." Here's a story that validates this in an interesting and life-saving way.

Dr. Bob Price of Tri-City Hospital sent me this little gem: One of the greatest success stories in the history of the United States in this century is the story of the Golden Gate Bridge. It was largely financed by Marin County and San Francisco, the two communities it eventually connected. Underneath the bridge there were two other "communities." One was a community of the men working on the bridge, and the other community was composed of men waiting for someone to get killed so they would have a job.

Sometimes the wait was not very long because during the first part of the construction of the Golden Gate Bridge, no safety devices were used, and twenty-three men fell to their deaths. For the last part of the project, however, a large net that cost $100,000 was employed. At least ten men fell into it, and their lives were spared. The interesting sidelight, however, is that 25 percent more work was accomplished when the men were assured of their safety. The

> *Fear—whether it is fear of falling, fear of failing, or fear of being found out—is a heavy burden to carry.*

25 percent increase in productivity paid for that safety net many times over, not to mention what it did for the men's families and the men whose lives were saved.

Both communities got what they wanted. Their magnificent bridge served a wonderful purpose, and they got it at a much-reduced price because they helped those workers get what they wanted—a safe, secure, well-paying job. Think about it. Buy that philosophy.

———————

Even on the springboard to success, you have to bounce a little.

"What I Do Is Who I Am"

*S*everal years ago I heard about an ad placed in a sports magazine advising hunters how not to scatter their shots. The ad said, "For one dollar we'll give you that information." Many people sent their dollar, and the advice was, "Just use one shot." Although the ad was deceptive, and I'm certain many of the respondents were irritated at being taken in, the advice was good.

A classic example of someone who did not scatter his shots is Chris Schenkel. Schenkel has been one of the most enduring sportscasters in history. For more than four decades, he has frequently been identified as the "good guy of sports." Schenkel is not putting on an act when he is identified as the good guy who looks for the good in others. Despite some criticism for being too liberal with praise and not critical or judgmental enough, Schenkel declares, "What I do is who I am."

> *Be yourself. You will make a lousy anybody else, but nobody else can be as good as you at being you.*

Chris Schenkel's dream to be a broadcaster started back in the 1930s. He listened to baseball games on the radio and studied the broadcasters' style. His dad purchased an early audio disc recorder for him. Chris recorded the games and practiced mimicking the announcer. When he was a freshman at Purdue University, Chris took a summer job at WLBC in Muncie, Indiana, for $18 a week. In 1952, he began as a substitute announcer for the ABC fights on radio. Later he was a substitute announcer for the New York Giants football games on TV. His goal always was to be the best he could be, using his abilities and being himself.

Today, Chris Schenkel is one of the most respected broadcasters in America, and he achieved that status by understanding who he was, being a good-finder, concentrating his efforts, and not scattering his shots. The message is clear: "What you do is who you are."

_____

No one appreciates the value of constructive criticism more thoroughly than the one who's giving it.

The Ten-Year-Old Entrepreneur

*M*arc Wright is a seasoned performer in the world of free enterprise and opportunity. He is the president of the Kiddie Card Company and one of the youngest entrepreneurs in Canada. Marc started his business when he was just six years old after listening to some motivational tapes. Following a visit to an art museum, Marc thought he would make some drawings and see if he could earn money. His mother suggested he put his pictures on cards and sell them. He was an immediate success with some rather unique concepts.

Ideas do not care about the age, sex, race, creed, or color of who has them or what someone does with them.

He knocks on the door (incidentally, his mom goes with him) and gives his short but effective sales talk. He introduces himself, "Hi. My name is Marc and I'm freezing! I'm selling greeting cards. How many would you like to buy? Here's a handful. Just pick the ones you want and pay me what you want." His cards are hand-drawn on pink, green, and white paper. They cover the seasons of the year, and Marc sells them about three days a week for a total of six or seven hours. He averages about seventy-five cents a card and sells about twenty-five cards in an hour.

Marc quickly realized he would need help, so he currently

has ten staff members, primarily artists who draw the pictures. He pays them a quarter for each original drawing. He has expanded his operation through the mail and seems to get busier and busier. His first year in business, Marc earned $3,000—enough to take his mom on a trip to Disney World.

By age ten, Marc had become something of a media celebrity. He appeared on *Late Night with David Letterman* and was interviewed by Conan O'Brien.

Marc had an idea, didn't count his birthdays, received some encouragement from his mother, and started his business. Question: Do you have an idea that's marketable? If you do, take action!

Home owner to TV repairman: "It goes out so often I call it 'Old Fadeful.'" (Bob Thaves, Newspaper Enterprise Association)

Manners Do Matter

*T*oday, we too rarely practice good manners. However, having good manners, including expressing gratitude, is a great asset. When we neglect to require our children to say "thank you" when somebody gives them a gift, says something nice about them, or does something for them, we are raising ungrateful children who are highly unlikely to be happy. Without gratitude, happiness is a rare thing. With gratitude, the odds go up dramatically that happiness will be the result.

A classic example of the validity of gratitude in action is the story of Roy Rogers. After he starred in his first movie, he began receiving huge stacks of fan mail that he wanted to answer. However, his salary of $150 a week did not even cover the required postage. He talked to the head of Republic Pictures in the hope that the studio would handle some of his fan mail. He was summarily turned down and told he was foolish to think about answering fan mail because nobody else did. It took too much time and money.

> *Gratitude is the healthiest of all human emotions.*
> —Hans Selje

Roy Rogers, one of the genuinely good guys of life, couldn't buy that. It was his conviction that if someone thought enough about him to write him a fan letter, he should have enough respect for the person to answer it. Fortunately, the movie that caused him his "problem" also made him so popular that he could go on a personal appearance tour. He traveled many miles and performed countless one-night stands to raise the money to pay the salaries of the four people it took to answer his fan mail.

As a result of answering each fan's letter, he built a fan base that was faithful to him and remains faithful to him many, many years later. Yup, the good guys and the good gals really do win. So, develop some manners, respect others, and be grateful for what you have.

I don't mind that my son is earning more than I did on my first job. What disturbs me is he's just six, and it's his allowance!

This Way to Happiness

Many years ago I heard the statement, "Happiness is not pleasure. It is victory." There is much truth in that.

Happiness, it is safe to assume, is something everybody wants to have. It's true that other people can give you pleasure, but you will never be happy until you do things for other people. Nothing brings more joy and happiness than doing things for others that increase their enjoyment of life. Incidentally, happiness is not something you can buy with money, though it is true that an adequate amount of money helps to eliminate some things that produce discomfort.

Studies reveal that people who are absorbed in tasks they enjoy and find challenging have taken a step toward happiness. Researchers have long recognized that people (particularly males) who are married are happier and live longer. People who are on a regular exercise program, keeping themselves physically in shape, particularly from an aerobic point of view, are happier.

> *The things that count most in life are the things that can't be counted.*

An article in *Psychology Today* specifically states that one way to be happy is to "take care of the soul." The article points out that actively religious people tend to report more happiness and to cope better with crises. Faith provides a support community, a sense of life's meaning, a reason to focus beyond self, and a timeless perspective on life's temporary ups and downs.

A study conducted by David Jensen at UCLA covering a broad range of people from every walk of life concluded that people who set goals and develop a plan of action to reach them are happier and healthier, earn considerably more money, and get along better with the people at home than do people who have no clearly defined objectives. Consider this happiness factor as you set your goals.

Junior executive to friend: "My boss and I never clash. He goes his way, and I go his." (Cincinnati Enquirer)

Life Is Like a Grindstone

I believe this title is true. Life really is like a grindstone in that it will either grind you down or polish you up. It seems that some people have bounced back from disaster, defeat, and virtually every imaginable form of difficulty. That is certainly the case with Iyanla Vanzant. According to an article in the June 28, 1995, issue of the *Dallas Morning News,* Iyanla was raped when she was just nine years old. She had a child at age sixteen and a nervous breakdown at age twenty-two. She spent eleven years on welfare.

Her will to win and a never-say-die spirit, combined with sacrifice, perseverance, and faith, have propelled Iyanla to the top. She earned a law degree and became a criminal defense attorney. Not only that, she is an author, a radio and television talk show host, and an inspirational

> *Wise are they who have learned these truths—trouble is temporary, time is a tonic, tribulation is a test tube.*
> —William Arthur Ward

speaker. Her universal message seems to tap back into the kind of spirituality that our grandmothers had. She is living proof that it is not where you start or even what happens to you along the way that's important. What is important is that you persevere and never give up on yourself.

She is an upbeat, enthusiastic, and optimistic person who delights in persuading others that they, too, can get it all together and do great things with their lives, regardless of what their past might have been. She knows and tells others that it's not easy, but she believes it can be done. I might add that I share that same conviction, so pick yourself up by your bootstraps, go to work with the right attitude, hang in there, and expect good things to happen.

———————————————

A man at the traffic-fine window in our local courthouse was obviously displeased as he paid his fine. When the clerk handed him a receipt, he growled, "What do I do with this?" "Keep it," said the clerk cheerfully. "When you get ten of them, you get a bicycle." (M. Dwight Bell)

Needed—One More Friend

Somebody remarked that a stranger is simply a friend you haven't met. My trusty 1828 Noah Webster dictionary says that a friend is one who is attached to another by affection, which leads him to desire his company, or one who has sufficient interest to serve another.

The dictionary definition amply describes Mike Corbett who, along with his friend Mark Wellman, on July 19, 1989, started the assault on El Capitan. El Capitan is a sheer rock wall 3,569 feet above the floor of Yosemite Valley in northern California. It is one of the most difficult mountains for rock climbers to scale. The combination of difficulty and danger is sufficient to test the strength and courage of even the world's most elite climbers.

It took Wellman and Corbett seven days to make the climb. They encountered temperatures of up to 105 degrees and wind gusts that made the ascent even more difficult. When they reached the summit, Corbett stood in triumph, but Wellman just kept his seat. Wellman is the first person to scale El Capitan without the use of his legs.

> *Life is an exciting business and most exciting when it is lived for others.*
> —Helen Keller

Wellman had given up climbing in 1982 after he was paralyzed as the result of a fall. From that point on the only rock climbing he did was in his dreams. Then Corbett convinced him they could climb the mountain together. Wellman certainly couldn't have done it without

Corbett, who led the way and helped Wellman move through each stage, higher and higher. Perhaps the pinnacle of friendship and courage was reached when on the seventh day Corbett was unable to secure the pitons in the loose rock skirting the summit. Knowing that a misstep would send them both plunging to their deaths, Corbett hoisted Wellman onto his back and clambered the remaining distance to the top.

An old but very true statement holds that if you would have a friend, be a friend. I encourage you to be a friend as Mike Corbett was to Mark Wellman.

———————

The secret of good management is to keep the guys who hate you away from the guys who are still undecided. (Casey Stengel)

My Most Unforgettable Character

*T*he Eartha White story appeared in *Reader's Digest* nearly forty years ago. She was the four-and-a-half-foot-tall daughter of a former slave. She believed that "service is the price we pay for the space we occupy on this planet." She lived by the principle that each of us should do all the good we can in all the ways we can in all the places we can for all the people we can while we can.

Miss Eartha gave up a promising opera career to join her mother in trying to make things easier for the people who came to her mother's free soup kitchen. She taught school for sixteen years, then used her small savings to open a department store that catered primarily to African-Americans. She eventually started a steam laundry, an employment agency, a real estate company, and an insurance business. She amassed an estate worth more than $1 million, only to commit most of it to projects that made her a one-woman welfare department.

Love your enemies. Without them you'd probably have nobody to blame but yourself.

Her life was about helping people. She reached down and lifted those who needed a hand up instead of a handout. She maintained a boarding home for indigents and a mercy hospital for those who had become completely helpless. At another house she took in unwed mothers, and in another she nursed alcoholics back to sobriety. She also donated buildings for two childcare centers and turned a vacant movie house into a recreation center for children who lived in slums. Her deep faith led her to quote John 15:7 (KJV), which says, "If ye abide in me, and my words abide in you, ye shall ask what ye will, and it shall be done unto you."

She worked hard, lived expectantly, and died fulfilled. If each of us did a fraction of what she did, the contribution to society would be significant. The sheer joy of giving and doing for others is hard to top. Take action. Follow Eartha White's example, and the road to the top will be smoother.

A sign at the beginning of the serving line in front of the apples at a church picnic: "God is watching, take only one." At the end of the line next to the cookies, a little sign said, "Take as many as you want. God is busy watchin' the apples."

It's Not Where You Start—It's Where You Go

Dave Longaberger graduated from high school at age twenty. He repeated first grade and three-peated fifth grade. He reads at the eighth-grade level, stutters, and has epilepsy. In 1996, his company, The Longaberger Company, sold more than $525 million in handmade baskets, pottery, fabric, and other home decor items through 36,000 independent sales consultants nationwide. How did it happen?

Dave has a lot of positives going for him. He possesses an entrepreneurial spirit. As a child, he worked so many jobs, his family called him the "twenty-five-cent millionaire." He learned many important lessons from his jobs. As a seven-year-old in a grocery store, he learned that the way to please the boss was to figure out what the boss wanted and get it done. Next, he studied people and learned about them from every job. Examples: Work could be fun, and he did a better job when he enjoyed his work. The more the people he dealt with liked him, the more likely they were to continue doing business with him.

> *Genius produces great ideas and concepts. Hard work produces the results.*

In the army he learned about uniformity, control, consistency, and Central Headquarters. He also learned how to become a risk taker and not a gambler. For example, he opened a tiny restaurant on a shoestring. On opening day he had $135 that he used to buy the first day's breakfast fixings. After breakfast, he had enough money to buy supplies for lunch, and then he used the money he made from lunch to buy dinner preparations. That's starting a business on bare bones!

Later, Dave bought a grocery store and ran it very successfully. All the time he was preparing for bigger and better things. His optimism, patience, and hard work enabled him to overcome many difficulties. We all can learn from the lessons that Dave learned on the way up. (To learn more about The Longaberger Company, see its Web page at www.longaberger.com.)

Remember, some of us learn from other people's mistakes and the rest of us have to be the other people.

One Incident Can Change Us Forever

*I*n the last century a rich boy and a poor boy lived in the same neighborhood. The rich boy wore nice clothes, lived in a nice house, and had plenty of good, nutritious food to eat. The poor boy lived in a cheap house, wore ragged clothes, and did not have much of anything to eat. One day the boys got into a scuffle. In the struggle the rich boy won. The poor boy got up, dusted himself off, and told the rich kid that if he had the proper food to eat as the rich boy did, he would have won. Then the poor boy turned and walked away. The rich kid just stood there. He was numbed by what the poor boy said. His heart was broken because he knew that it was true.

The rich boy never forgot that experience. From that day on he revolted against any favored treatment because he was rich. He made it a point to wear inexpensive clothing; he intentionally endured the hardships faced by people who were poor. His family was often embarrassed by the way he dressed, but despite family pressure, the young boy never again took advantage of his wealth.

> *Our purpose in life should be to see one another through, not through one another.*

History omits the name of the poor boy, but the rich boy who developed such compassion for poor people made them his life's work. His name is recorded in history. He dedicated his life to service and became a world-class physician, serving in Africa. His name was Albert Schweitzer.

I'm not suggesting that we all be as selfless as Albert Schweitzer, but I do believe that we need to be more in tune with the thinking and feelings of others. Very few people have had as much impact on the world as Albert Schweitzer did. Even fewer people have gotten as much satisfaction out of life as he did.

An optimist is a person who will use his last dollar to buy a money belt.

Improbable, Impossible, and Can't Happen

*H*e started his career on the Senior PGA Tour wearing tennis shoes and $2 pants. He had no glove. He carried a $20 golf bag and a $70 set of clubs. He is potbellied, has long sideburns, and plays with a wide stance and a strong right grip. He holds his hands high and away and uses about a three-quarter swing. (That's not the way the PGA pros teach the game.)

I've just described one of the latest additions to the Senior PGA Tour. Robert Landers, at age fifty, has to be the most improbable candidate to ever make the touring pros' prestigious seniors tournament schedule. A movie scriptwriter could never have sold this one to Hollywood. Robert started playing at age twenty-two and entered his first tournament at twenty-eight. Between 1983 and 1991, back problems prevented him from playing or practicing the game he loved. Since then he has played only an average of once a week. He is completely self-taught. He has never read a golf book or taken a lesson.

> *Run your day by the clock and your life with a vision, and you will cause good things to happen.*

This golfer has had more than his share of ups and downs. The store where he worked earning $18,000 a year went out of business, and he lost his job. He helped make ends meet by cutting and selling firewood and in the process strengthened his hands. He has a small farm and has been practicing by hitting golf balls over his barn and over his cows. He cashed in $4,000 of a $10,000 IRA in order to finance his trip to Florida to qualify for the tour. Amazingly enough, he made it.

Message: Robert Landers had a dream—a most improbable one. He made the commitment to go for it and took advantage of every opportunity to practice and prepare for the challenge. He avoided the P.L.O.M. ("Poor Little Ol' Me") disease and capitalized on his natural ability and winning attitude. Who knows? Maybe the same approach will work for you as you pursue your dream.

Childhood is a time of rapid changes. Between the ages of twelve and seventeen a parent can age thirty years! (Sam Levenson)

Do Long Hours Guarantee More Productivity and More Profit?

*M*aybe. Maybe not. In a *Wall Street Journal* article, industrial psychologist John Kamp said, "Everybody's got a different limit. But there's a point for every person at which extra hours cause a drop in work quality and an increase in stress." There seems to be a fine line between the extra productivity created by the extra hours and a decline in the quality and creativity of the finished product of those extra hours.

In addition, the number one cause of the productivity decline in America is marital difficulty, according to an article in *USA Today*. It seems likely that many people who work long hours in an effort to be more productive actually harm their productivity and their marriages at the same time. People who work too many hours may also lose their ability to appreciate and achieve the goals of their employer. "We want to make sure people see how their efforts fit into the big picture," says Kirby Dyess, vice president of human resources for Intel.

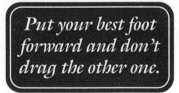

Put your best foot forward and don't drag the other one.

Intel is also wary of overwork intruding on workers' personal lives. In surveys over the past few years, Ms. Dyess says, Intel employees who report success in balancing their professional and personal obligations were more likely to say they could tolerate competitive pressures (such as ambiguity and change) than those who said work dominated their lives.

An internal study showed no correlation between hours worked and advancement at Intel. Education, experience, and results matter more. However, Ms. Dyess says there are times when it makes sense to work extra hours. Maury Hanigan, a New York consultant who advises companies on personnel strategies, says in a new job "you need to put in the time to get up to speed and make your mark," perhaps for a year.

Your personal, family, and business lives are *all* important, and astute leaders and managers are sensitive to that fact. The best way to be successful is to maintain that balance.

Running into debt doesn't bother some people, but running into their creditors really upsets them.

The Fully Equipped Cow

*T*he story is told about a farmer who went into an automobile dealership to buy a stripped-down model and ended up with all the bells and whistles. The $14,000 standard car turned into a $22,000 luxury vehicle. He loved all the extras, but frankly, he had exceeded his budget. A few months later he had a chance to at least partially balance the scale. The salesman who sold him the car showed up at his farm to buy a cow. After carefully looking the herd over, he made his choice and asked, "How much?"

Great things are accomplished with slow movement. Nothing is accomplished by standing still.

The farmer pleasantly replied that the price was $395. The salesman was pleased and said he would take the cow. The farmer went into his shed, figured the details, came back out, and presented the salesman with the bill totaling $920.20. Needless to say, the salesman responded with some feeling, "But I thought you told me the price was $395!" The farmer assured him that was the price of the standard cow, but this one came equipped with a two-tone genuine leather cowhide cover for an additional $95. There was an extra stomach built in to increase capacity and performance, which was $110. The attached flyswatter was $35, and at $15 each the four milk dispensers came to an extra $60. The colorful dual horns at $20 each came to $40, and the automatic fertilizer plant, guaranteed for life, was another $125, for a total of $465. The tax was $60.20, so the total bill was $920.20.

I'm certain many of you, as you read this, feel a degree of empathy with the farmer. Maybe the smile you get from the story and the fact that you can share it with others will reduce some of the pain that goes, on occasion, with overspending your budget. Go ahead. Have a good laugh. Share it with others.

The last thing my kids ever did to earn money was lose their baby teeth. (Phyllis Diller, "Rod's Ponders," May 16, 1994)

Reward Yourself

*T*he late William Arthur Ward was and is one of my favorite writers. His insights and ability to put a philosophy of life into a few words were truly remarkable. Here is a sample from his book *Reward Yourself*:

> A man phoned his physician and excitedly exclaimed: "Please come at once, Doctor. My son has swallowed my fountain pen."
>
> The doctor replied, "I'll be right over. But what are you doing in the meanwhile?"
>
> "Using a pencil," answered the father.
>
> What we do "in the meanwhile" is of vital importance to our lives—and to the lives of others. What we do with our leisure time can build our character or destroy it. It can make our fortune or mar it.
>
> While we wait for a traffic light to change, we can pray for our president, our nation, and the world.
>
> While we wait for an elevator we can be still and know that God is, and that He is still in charge of the universe.
>
> While we drive or ride to work, we can affirmatively and joyously meditate on that which is true, pure, lovely, and positive.
>
> While we wash dishes, mow the lawn, or perform other tasks that require less than our complete attention, we can sing, whistle, or hum the tunes of great songs and hymns that

Speaking of "mere words" is like speaking of "mere dynamite."

inevitably make life more beautiful for us and for our fellow human beings.

While we sit in the waiting room of our physician or dentist, we can thank God for dedicated professional people, and we can pray for those patients who might be anxious, fearful, despondent, or in pain.

What we do with our golden "in the meanwhile" moments can enrich and inspire, encourage and uplift, bless and brighten our important corner of the world.

These are more than words on a piece of paper—they present a philosophy of life. Adopt it for your own, and you truly will reward yourself.

Man to friend: "I figured out why inflation is still here. Everybody's earning money five days a week, but the government is spending it seven days a week." (Don Reber in the Reading, Pennsylvania, *Times*)

Be Kind and Listen

A wise person said that it's nice to be important, but it's more important to be nice. Another "oldie" is that when you're talking, you're not learning; it's only when you listen that you learn.

Listening will avoid some embarrassments and might even make you some money. For example, when Tommy Bolt was on the golf tour, he established a well-deserved reputation for his temper. His breaking and throwing of clubs became locker-room fodder and a topic for media discussion. Once in a tournament, he drew a caddie who had a reputation for being a talker, so Bolt told him to keep quiet and restrict his conversation to "Yes, Mr. Bolt" or "No, Mr. Bolt."

Temper is far too valuable to lose, so watch yours carefully and you probably won't lose it.

As luck would have it, one of Bolt's shots stopped close to a tree. To reach the green, he had to hit the ball under a branch and over a lake. He carefully analyzed the situation and made a decision. However, as it frequently happens, halfway talking to his caddie and halfway talking to himself, he asked, "Should I hit it with my five iron?" The caddie, having been duly warned, responded, "No, Mr. Bolt." Bolt's temper and pride prompted him to say, "What do you mean, not a five iron? Just watch this shot!" The caddie, still following instructions, said, "No, Mr. Bolt!" Bolt wasn't listening. He took dead aim and hit the shot beautifully to the green. It stopped a couple of feet from the hole. With a look of self-satisfaction, Bolt handed the caddie his five iron and commented, "What do you think about that? And it's okay for you to talk now." "Mr. Bolt, that wasn't your ball," the caddie responded.

Hitting the wrong ball cost Tommy Bolt a two-shot penalty and lots of money. Message: Be nice to people, especially those who serve you, and listen to what they have to say.

Nothing confuses a man more than to drive behind a woman who does everything right.

Inspiring Teachers Produce Inspired Students

Ms. Romayne Welch from the Reynolds Elementary School in Baldwinsville, New York, is a truly outstanding teacher. She is an example of what dedication, inspiration, a love for children, and a commitment to excellence will produce. This dedicated teacher and her students are very creative. They see an opportunity in every problem. During the 1993 school session, they produced a magnificent opera, *Creating Original Opera*. Can you imagine nine- and ten-year-olds writing, producing, and performing in their own opera, and having a fifth grader as the orchestra conductor? Ms. Welch said the most difficult part for her was "letting go and allowing the kids to make and carry through on their decisions."

The class was allotted only $125 for the entire production, and the footlight supplies alone cost that much. They turned their creativity to a fund-raiser and produced an additional $1,200 that they needed. The kids in the second through fifth grades made five sets of note cards in packages of six each. They designed them with musical symbols, and they were outstanding! Furthermore, since an opera

> *Inside every person there are seeds of greatness. The responsibility of parents and leaders is to nurture and cultivate those seeds.*

needs box seats, the kids made seats out of boxes. It was hilarious.

The bottom line is, the opera was quite successful, and it planted the seed for other projects—including a musical about immigration and Ellis Island. I have an idea that whatever Ms. Welch and her students attack will be successful and the kids will have many other growth opportunities. They will also have marvelous opportunities to show what talented, directed young people can do.

More of us need to get involved in working with our young people instead of being so quick to criticize. Congratulations to you, Ms. Romayne Welch, and all those outstanding students at Reynolds Elementary School. Here's hoping parents and teachers all over America will take a page from your notebook and direct their students into more activities of a similar nature. These activities will enable them to turn their creative energy into character- and confidence-building projects.

———————

My doctor gave me six months to live. When I told him I couldn't pay the bill, he gave me six more months. (Walter Matthau)

Reading, Writing, and Arithmetic—Not Enough

*D*on't misunderstand—the need for these three skills is so obvious that in our ever-increasingly complex world they don't merit discussion. However, according to John Stinson, vice president of human resources at Trans-Canada PipeLines Limited, we've got to go much farther than these basic skills. He points out that goal setting, self-esteem, ethics, learning the language of your business, respecting diversity, integrity, persistence, teamwork, time management, and problem solving are all components that cannot be overlooked.

This will necessitate change in our thinking, and change always involves stress. Stinson maintains, "If you don't have the ability to handle change and move on, you're going to be in trouble." The need for change increases as the world changes, and the needs of our customers change accordingly. The employee must change by growing in skills and willingness to adapt.

Consider this: From 1972 until 1991, American exports of automobiles to Japan declined roughly 2 percent. German exports of automobiles to Japan in the same time period increased

> *Our words reveal our thoughts—manners mirror our self-esteem. Our actions reflect our character; our habits predict the future.*
> —William Arthur Ward

more than 700 percent, and Germans worked under the same restraints as Americans did. Here's the difference: The Germans recognized that the Japanese drive on the left-hand side of the road, the steering wheel is on the right side of the car, and their cars are much smaller. Solution: Put the steering wheel on the right, make the cars smaller, and the Japanese will buy them. When the American Jeep Cherokee, built to meet Japanese wishes, arrived in 1992, it was an immediate hit in Japan. Message: Prepare yourself to meet the needs of the marketplace, and I can assure you that employers will be looking for you—particularly if you're really good at what you've prepared yourself to do.

When better money is made, college students will write home for it.

She Gave Everything She Had

*T*oscanini said that Marian Anderson had the sweetest voice "this side of heaven." She sang before royalty and heads of governments in the opera houses of Europe and America. She had an extraordinary vocal range, going from soprano to the lowest contralto with a pure tone.

Marian Anderson got her start by scrubbing floors for ten cents an hour so that she could buy a pawnshop violin. The church she attended recognized her rare talent and raised money for a professional voice teacher to work with her. When the teacher pronounced her ready, she went to New York where critics crucified her. She returned home to regroup. Her mother and her church encouraged her and paid for more lessons.

That time, because of the intense racial prejudice in America, she went to Europe and took the Continent by storm. She came back to America and sang at the Lincoln Memorial with more than sixty thousand people in attendance. She sang "O Mia Fernando," "Ave Maria," "Gospel Train," "Trampin'," and "My Soul Is Anchored in the Lord," among other songs. Those who were privileged to hear both her singing and Martin Luther King Jr. giving his "I Have a Dream" speech say that her music was even more moving than his oratory.

> *Remember, "The fruit we grow in the valleys of despair is the food we will eat on the mountaintop."*
> —Fred Smith

One day a reporter asked her what the most satisfying moment in her life was. Without hesitation, she responded that her most satisfying moment came when she was able to tell her mother that she did not have to take in any more washing. Her honors were too numerous to mention, and yet that was her most satisfying moment. The reporter asked her, "What did your mother give you?" Marian Anderson responded, "Everything she had."

That's greatness, and giving everything we have is our key to greatness.

The first and last completely accurate weather forecast was when God told Noah that it was going to rain.

One Basket at a Time

Many years ago when he was in the Orient, Bill Schiebler of Eden Prairie, Minnesota, had a unique experience. He was in farming country where every inch of ground is important. A towering hill with a bamboo thicket on top was part of the terrain. The elders of the village decided that the hill needed to be removed for farming purposes. The American mind could not conceive of the hill being moved without the aid of giant earthmoving equipment, but the Oriental mind and work ethic are different.

Thousands of people who lived in the immediate area participated in the venture and even accepted it as a routine matter of their everyday life. Baskets of dirt were handed down from top to bottom, and in some cases, the lines were two miles long. It appeared as if nothing was happening; the hill did not seem to be going away. But over a period of time, because of incredible teamwork, the commitment of thousands of people, and a steady day-by-day involvement, the hill gradually diminished and the lower areas rose to a beautiful, flat farming area.

The Americans who witnessed the effort were astonished because the day came when no hill was left. They realized then that virtually any task can be accomplished when you get everybody on the same page, committed to a joint effort for the mutual benefit of all. Bill Schiebler wisely makes the point that we should use this

> *Community should be spelled "come in unity."*

example for everyday living. When we are confronted with seemingly impossible tasks, if we break them down into small segments—or one basket at a time—we can literally accomplish the impossible and move those mountains. Note: The villagers took a liability (for farming purposes)—a mountain—and used that dirt to create a valuable asset (rich farmland).

Think about it. Examine your liabilities—maybe you can convert them to assets, even if it's just a basket at a time.

A prizefighter, floored in the second round by a powerful punch, tried to look up from the mat. "Let the referee count," yelled his trainer. "Don't get up until eight." The fighter nodded and replied weakly, "What time is it now?" (Executive Speechwriter Newsletter)

Part-Timer Makes It Big-Time

*W*hen Dean Sanders was a college student, he went to work part-time with Sam's Wholesale Warehouse. Today, he is the president of the company, which does in the neighborhood of $25 billion in business each year. I met and came to know Dean when I was speaking for Sam's grand opening of new stores.

One morning it was my pleasure to address Sam's staff at a breakfast before they opened for business. Dean's openness with his staff, his "shirtsleeve" approach, and his friendliness were refreshing, but I was really impressed when I noticed that Dean was moving some empty plates and cups to the trash barrel. As I observed him, I wondered how many presidents of $25 billion corporations would be doing such a thing. First, would they be at a working breakfast; second, would they mingle so easily and freely with the staff, which included highly paid executives and hourly wage earners; third, would they be cleaning up the breakfast dishes when so many other people were around?

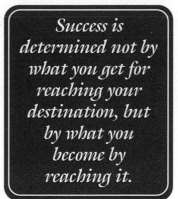

Success is determined not by what you get for reaching your destination, but by what you become by reaching it.

The thing that struck me is that Dean did it so matter-of-factly without giving it any obvious thought or the feeling, "Well, somebody's gotta do this and nobody else is doing it, so I suppose I will." It was an attitude of it was there; it needed doing; he was the closest and therefore the most logical one to do it.

It's true: "He who is greatest among you shall be your servant" (Matt. 23:11 NKJV). Today, many people think others should serve them, but the reality is that those who serve best are those who will lead the most. Think about it. Adopt the servant's attitude (without being servile).

———————

Columnist Ray Ratto in the San Francisco Examiner *on a potential problem facing the 49ers: "Carmen Policy is a lawyer. Steve Young is a lawyer. Center Bart Oats is a lawyer. Mark Trestman, the 49ers new offensive coordinator, is a lawyer. God help us all if they ever disagree on third and eight."*

It's Better to Give

*W*hen Wally Jansen told me about my new company's Christmas 'trip to the island' tradition," says Phillip Kelly, "I was intrigued. Ten days before Christmas the two hundred Puerto Rican families in this particular parish would gather and each family would place five dollars in the 'pot,' which was about a day's pay for a fruit picker back then. Each family would write its name on a slip of paper. Then they would blindfold someone to draw the name of the family that would get to go home for Christmas—two glorious weeks on the island, and enough money to buy Christmas presents for everyone. I went to the drawing that year, my first Christmas with the community, but it was going to be Wally Jansen's last. Wally was retiring after working forty years with the company, and for the last twenty-five he had been the canning factory foreman.

> *Truly successful people in life are givers and forgivers.*

"By three o'clock everyone had parted with their five dollars and the announcer called the committee onstage to witness the drawing. Then they called me up to draw the name of the lucky family. On went the blindfold and I was led to the drum. I reached in, sorted out a handful, and finally settled on one. I opened the slip of paper and read, 'Wally Jansen.' The cheers were deafening. Everyone surrounded him, hugging him, crying, congratulating him, wishing him a Merry Christmas and a joyous trip. While the commotion continued I casually reached back into the drum and drew out a handful of slips and opened a couple. Each one, in different writing, carried the same name—Wally Jansen."

I imagine that the Wally Jansen family was thrilled beyond words, but I believe the joy that each person felt, thinking that maybe he or she had written the name "Wally Jansen," which was drawn, was greater still. Think about that. Become a giver, and you will be happier on your trip to the top.

———

I heard about a fellow who found a note at home from his wife saying that she was suddenly called out of town but that he was going to love his dinner for the evening. He would find it on page 28 of the cookbook.

It's Not My Fault

*C*elebrated historian Barbara Tuchman called our times "the Age of Disruption." She said we have lost belief in certain kinds of morals and our understanding of good and bad is distorted. This two-time Pulitzer Prize–winner said that what we most need in the next century is "probably personal responsibility." She explained that taking responsibility for your behavior and your performance is not forever supposing that society must forgive you because it's "not your fault."

Ms. Tuchman was echoing many of society's sentiments. The "it's not my fault" cry is heard everywhere. It perhaps originates in childhood when siblings get into a squabble, and each proclaims, "It's not my fault!" The 1828 Noah Webster dictionary defines *fault* as "a failing, hence an error or mistake, a blunder, a defect." That definition helps explain why many people do not want to accept fault, choosing instead to deny it.

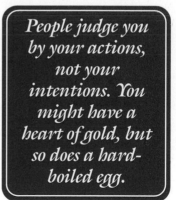

People judge you by your actions, not your intentions. You might have a heart of gold, but so does a hard-boiled egg.

When we see an altercation on an athletic field, the athletes generally point the finger of blame at someone else. We see it in the courts of law. The Menendez brothers explained that because their parents treated them brutally, they "had" to kill them. In Dallas when a young man killed two of his cousins, it was explained away as the "urban survival syndrome," a "kill or be killed" mentality. Thieves say, "It's not my fault—I couldn't get a job." The list is endless.

Realistically, until we accept responsibility for our actions, we will have little hope for our future. Message: The best way to live a fulfilled life is to accept responsibility for our performance and our actions. So start taking responsibility for your actions today, and soon it will become a way of life—and a much-improved life at that!

———

A five-year-old confidently told Art Linkletter that the chicken came before the egg because "God doesn't lay eggs."

Let's Hear It for Brenda Reyes and the Marine Corps

*L*aurie Wilson, in an article in the *Dallas Morning News,* identifies Brenda Reyes as the Texas Business Woman of the Year, a recognition of the Texas Association of Mexican American Chambers of Commerce. The 9,000-member group annually honors a businesswoman for her financial success, community involvement, and professional service.

Ms. Reyes is an independent businesswoman who owns Innovative Computer Group. Her first venture into the business world involved a short period of employment in a bank, but she quickly decided that wasn't her niche after she met a woman who had been performing the same task there every day for forty years. She enrolled in the University of New Orleans, then decided to enlist in the marines. She later returned to finish college.

In addition to the many lessons in honor and discipline she learned in the Marine Corps, her tour gave her the incentive to search for and capitalize on her strengths. After college, she recognized her aptitude for computers so in her spare time, she set up computer systems for friends who had lost patience with the process. At first she volunteered to help others, but soon she realized she could turn her knowledge into a career.

> *Consider the turtle. The only time it makes progress is when it sticks its neck out.*

She opened her first software development business in 1986 in her hometown of New Orleans and later moved her company to Dallas.

As a Marine Corps veteran, she has faced some tough situations and some hard-core marines, so making the presentation of her electronic document imaging equipment to a roomful of high-dollar executives doesn't really faze her. And as she points out, she doesn't have to salute. She has kept pace with all of the technological changes, she has courageously moved to expand her business, and the results are obvious by her recognition as Texas Business Woman of the Year. Congratulations, Brenda Reyes! You've set a good example and taught all of us a lesson in using what we have to its greatest advantage.

If Patrick Henry thought taxation without representation was bad, he should see it with representation.

Little Things Do Make Big Differences

*I*f my watch is four minutes slow and I show up for a noon flight at 12:04 P.M., you know what will happen. I have an arrangement with the airlines that if I'm not there when my flight is scheduled to leave, they are to go ahead and leave without me. They have always lived up to their end of the agreement.

Somebody once said that honesty in little things is no little thing. Also, the smallest good deed is better than the grandest intention. How right these statements are. On the serious side, a little thing can be enormously significant. Retired Brigadier General Robinson Risner was a

Open your eyes and you will undoubtedly see a hundred things you can and should express gratitude for. Do it.

prisoner of war in North Vietnam for more than seven years. He was in solitary confinement for five of those years. He suffered from cold, heat, malnutrition, and lack of fresh air. He was totally deprived of any human comfort. He jogged in his cell by the hour. When he became so frustrated he had to scream, he stuffed his underwear into his mouth to muffle the scream. He would not give his captors the satisfaction of knowing his frustration.

One day, in the depths of despair, General Risner lay down

on the floor and looked all around his small rectangular-shaped cell. He put his eye next to the cinder blocks, hoping that there would be a crack in one of them. Fortunately, there was a minute opening and he saw a single leaf. Later he stated that seeing that evidence of life outside was a tremendously uplifting and life-changing event.

When I heard his story, most of my complaints in life suddenly fell into context, and I resolved to be more appreciative of the many blessings I had instead of complaining about what I did not have. Fact: A quiet glance around you will reveal many blessings that you have already received and will continue to receive. Expressing appreciation for these blessings is a winning approach to life.

———

Diner: "I can't eat this soup." Waiter: "Sorry, sir, I'll call the manager." Diner: "Mr. Manager, I can't eat this soup." Manager: "I'll call the chef." Diner: "Mr. Chef, I can't eat this soup." Chef: "What's wrong with it?" Diner: "Nothing. I haven't got a spoon."

I'm the Only One Who Does Anything Around Here!

*S*everal years ago I was to appear on a late-night television show in New York City. For some strange reason, they wanted me in the studio that afternoon at 4:30. I walked in and was stunned by the small size of the reception area. It contained a couch for three, a chair for one, a sink, a refrigerator, and a coffeemaker.

As I sat down, a woman walked in, shook her head, and said, "Nobody makes any coffee except me!" She got busy and started a fresh pot of coffee. A few minutes later a guy walked in and, following the same procedure, said, "I can't believe it! This place would be a pigpen if it weren't for me! I'm the only person who ever does any cleanup." And he cleaned up the small area. Still later another woman walked in and complained, "Nobody ever puts anything up but me," and she proceeded to put things away.

> *Deal as gently with the faults of others as you do with your own.*
>
> —Chinese proverb

All three of those people sincerely felt they were the only ones who ever did anything. Each one did a private halo adjustment in going through the process of making up, cleaning up, or putting up.

Question: Is that the way it is in your company, where "nobody does anything," but everybody thinks he or she is the only one who actually works? Thought: If that is true and you are the only one who does anything, think of the incredible advantage that gives you. Not only do you have job security, but you have unlimited opportunity to move up the ladder. However, if you have a chip on your shoulder, if you honestly feel that you do everything and you share that feeling with others, your bad attitude negates your good work. So, stay busy, keep working, and smile about it. Your performance *and* good attitude about doing everything will catch up with you. You'll move up.

It's hard to say when one generation ends and the next begins—but it's somewhere around 9 or 10 at night. (*Executive Speechwriter Newsletter*)

A Team of All-Stars or an All-Star Team?

*I*n July of 1991, my wife and I were in Sydney, Australia. We had an opportunity to attend a performance of the Sydney Philharmonic Orchestra at the famed Opera House. The seats were choice, and our night was free, so we jumped at the opportunity. When we arrived thirty minutes early, the orchestra members were already warming up. The individuals came in all sizes, ages, and colors; there were both males and females. Some of them, such as the cymbalist, would perform five or six seconds during the entire evening, while the cellist had one part that would extend more than twenty minutes. As they warmed up, the music sounded like noise to me.

At one minute before eight the conductor walked onto the stage. Immediately, everybody sat up straight. As he stepped onto the riser, everybody came to attention. At eight o'clock, he raised the baton, and when his arms came down, the music started. What had been noise a few seconds earlier became a beautiful melody.

> *People have a way of becoming what you encourage them to be—not what you nag them to be.*

The orchestra leader had converted a team of all-stars to an all-star team. Although each instrument produced entirely different tones, they all blended together in harmony. No one instrument dominated any other; rather, each harmonized with and became a part of the others. Can you imagine what the results would have been had every artist made up his or her mind that his or her instrument should be the star of the performance?

The conductor had, for a number of years, been a musician in an orchestra. He had learned to be obedient and follow the orchestra conductor when he was a performer. In short, he had learned to obey so that later he could command. I once saw a young man with a T-shirt emblem proclaiming, "I follow no one." What a tragedy! Because until he learns to follow, he will never be able to lead.

A small child pointed to a picture and asked the policeman if it really was the picture of the most wanted person. "Yes," answered the policeman. "Well," inquired the youngster, "why didn't you keep him when you took his picture?" (The Rotarian)

Revitalizing Older Citizens

*I*n an exciting article in *U.S. News & World Report,* Joannie M. Schrof shares some encouraging information with the older citizens of America. She cites numerous studies on aging that I find very promising. She quotes from Harvard psychologist Douglas Powell's book, *Profiles in Cognitive Aging.* He says that one-fourth to one-third of subjects in their eighties performed as well as younger counterparts. Even the lowest scorers suffered only modest declines.

Research indicates that exercise is the factor that seems most likely to benefit the brainpower of the healthy, sick, young, and old alike. Moderate exercise, such as thirty minutes of walking a day, is very beneficial. Perhaps the best news is that even if you temporarily lose part of your mental capacity, you might be able to regain it. An older brain retains an astonishing ability to rejuvenate itself. Stanley Rapoport, chief of the neuroscience lab at the National Institute on Aging, compares the brains of younger and older people engaged in the same efforts with amazing results. He finds that older brains literally rewire themselves to compensate for losses. If one neuron isn't up to the job, neighboring brain cells pick up the slack.

> *When retirement is mentioned in the Bible, it is always a punishment.*

One intriguing study by Harvard's Ellen Langer and Rebecca Levy suggests that cultural norms may be self-fulfilling prophecies. In China, where age carries no connotation of stupor, older people perform much higher on tests than their American counterparts. In short, your attitude and expectations are determining factors in your capacity as you grow older. Another exciting plus is that older people consistently outshine younger people on all measures of wisdom, offering more thoughtful, sophisticated advice.

But the best news of all is that you can do some things to enliven your brain: (1) Be flexible; (2) find peace; (3) eat right; (4) get lots of stimulation; (5) stay in school; (6) seek new horizons; (7) engage the world; (8) take a daily walk; and (9) keep control. So take the active, positive approach now and enjoy a mentally alert senior citizen's life.

———————

Remember, you're a part of the business you work for just as much as a bass drum is a part of the orchestra. Likewise, don't forget that bass drum solos are highly monotonous.

From Wealth to Broke to Wealth

*W*hen Castro and his Communist regime took over Cuba, the socialist system replaced free enterprise, and many successful people were devastated. Carlos Arboleya, an accounts officer for one of the largest banks in Cuba, was one of them. In 1960, shortly after Castro took over, Carlos arrived at work and discovered that the Communists had taken over all private banks. Three weeks later he was able to get himself, his wife, and his small son out of Cuba. The only problem was, Carlos arrived in America with only $42 in cash. He was unemployed, had no place to stay, and did not know a single person in Miami. He sought employment by going to every bank in Miami, but all of them turned him down. He finally found a job in a shoe factory, taking inventory.

Carlos worked with enthusiasm and with enormous energy

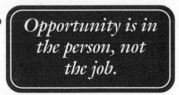

Opportunity is in the person, not the job.

as he put in countless extra hours. Results were spectacular, and within sixteen months he was manager of the shoe company. A short time later he was offered a job at the bank where the shoe company did business. From there he moved into the presidency of the largest chain of banks in America.

Carlos Arboleya did what he had to do (provide for his family) by taking a job he was overqualified for and eventually landed the job he desired. He proved that it is not *where* you start but *that* you start that counts. Speaker Joe Sabah puts it this way: "You don't have to be great to start, but you have to start to be great."

Carlos's story is a vignette in the overall picture of America. It's the land where anyone who will apply himself or herself, and grow in the job, can move forward to unique successes. This is evidenced by the fact that 80 percent of all millionaires in America are first-generation Americans. Think about it, give it your best shot, and your success chances increase dramatically.

———————

My doctor told me my appendix had to come out. When I demanded a second opinion he said, "That is my second opinion. At first I thought it was your kidney." (Gary Apple)

Those "Instant" Successes

Many times an unknown person does something spectacular and suddenly becomes a hero, a public figure, an overnight success, the object of much envy. Let's explore this "overnight success" syndrome, which almost always occurs over time.

Several years ago Gary Spiess from White Lake, Minnesota, did an incredible thing. He sailed his ten-foot boat across the Atlantic Ocean in just fifty-four days. Most of us can only imagine what he endured to complete his fifty-four-day ordeal, but suddenly, the whole world knew who he was.

What is the real story? Did he just have a good idea, implement it, and "luck" into celebrity status? Gary worked, planned, sacrificed, and studied for three years to build his boat. He committed not only his money but also 100 percent of his spare time for three solid years. He had to chart his course and plan every detail, including maximum use of his space and the proper food, clothing, and water to carry.

> *Those who stand out from the crowd have learned that all development is self-development.*

Once the trip began, so did the danger. The most dangerous and difficult part was fighting the violent seas of the Atlantic Ocean. The seas often combined with a driving, bitterly cold rain, which chilled him to the bone. By the time he reached England, he was so brutally battered by the cruel sea that his entire body was black and blue. Yes, he had his day in the sun, but it's safe to say that he sacrificed and worked in order to receive his rewards.

Most of us are not interested in doing anything of that nature, but it's safe to say that if we're going to accomplish anything of significance, and particularly if we're going to maintain that significance, long hours of planning and even more hours of hard work are required. It's also safe to say it's worth it because the effort is temporary, but the satisfaction and rewards can be long-lasting.

A man loaned his best friend five thousand dollars for plastic surgery. Unfortunately, he will never recover it because now he can't recognize him.

Love Is a Score in Tennis

*L*ove is also something you do for other people. It's an active verb. Speaking of active, well into his seventies and despite two knee operations, James Lewis is continuing his lifelong practice of teaching Alabama youngsters to play tennis. *Sports Illustrated* told his story in a special feature. He is a retired African-American steelworker who grew up in segregated Birmingham. As a child, he was not allowed to play tennis in the public parks. However, the old saying, "Where there's a will, there's a way," held true. James played under circumstances he created. He carved out a red clay court on a vacant lot and painted lines on vacant concrete wherever he could find it.

More than just a legend in his own time, James Lewis thoroughly enjoys teaching kids how to solve the mysteries of the game. In the process, he teaches them a lot more than tennis; he leads by example, teaching them sportsmanship and how to compete successfully against all odds. They learn that tennis is fun.

As a youngster, he loved to hit tennis balls, and he seemed to have a natural ability for the game. He taught himself to play and immediately started teaching others. He teaches that tennis is a

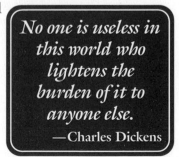

No one is useless in this world who lightens the burden of it to anyone else.

—Charles Dickens

step-by-step progression, "Forehand, backhand, volley, serve." Once students learn that, he lets them try to put it all together, "just like a jigsaw puzzle." "He truly is one of the most loving, unselfish men you will find, sharing everything from his time and knowledge to his equipment and even his food," says Louis Hill, director of tennis in suburban Fairfield, Alabama.

Several of Lewis's students have won college scholarships. These days, Lewis focuses his missionary zeal on several recreational programs—one of which is named for him—and two local colleges. He is a real go-giver who is winning by creating winners. Try James Lewis's approach to life.

Emcee: "I'm not too good at making introductions, but that's all right because our next guest is not so good at making speeches."

"She Was Speed and Motion Incarnate"

*T*he title above is a quote by Jesse Owens. He was speaking of Wilma Rudolph, who was born prematurely, the twentieth of twenty-two children. As a young child, she contracted double pneumonia and scarlet fever. At age four, she developed polio, and her left leg began to atrophy. The doctors thought she would never walk again, but her family didn't give up. They took turns massaging her legs for hours. Finally, with the aid of a brace and orthopedic shoe, she slowly started to walk. She had been bedridden and out of school for two years.

When she was eleven, the leg brace came off, and the orthopedic shoe, which she hated, was thrown away. Wilma Rudolph was free at last.

Wilma had an absolute passion for running. She would occasionally skip school and sneak into a local stadium. The sheer joy of running was so great that she would run all day long. Within a year she was challenging the boys in the neighborhood and beating most of them. At age fifteen, just four years after she threw away the brace, she was invited by Ed Temple to train with the Tigerbelles, the celebrated Tennessee State University women's track team. At age sixteen, she qualified for the 1956 Olympic team but won only a bronze medal. She then enrolled at Tennessee State on a track scholarship and trained

> *You can't climb the ladder of success with cold feet.*

under Ed Temple, who coached the '60 Olympic team. On that team Wilma became a superstar. On the day before her first heat in the 100, she severely sprained her ankle but still won gold medals in the 100 meter and the 200 meter. She then anchored the 400-meter relay en route to her third gold medal.

What Wilma Rudolph did was incredible! I believe her success was not in spite of her problems, but because of them. She treasured the good health that others took for granted. Her joy filled her with an exuberance that intensified her training and enabled her to outshine the athletes of her day. Think about it. Follow your star, and chances are good you will reach new heights.

You wonder if a fish goes home and exaggerates the size of the bait it stole.

All of Us Are in Debt

*A*lbert Einstein said, "A hundred times every day I remind myself that my inner and outer life are based on the labors of other men living and dead, and that I must exert myself in order to give in the same measure as I have received." As you think about what Einstein said, you will come to realize the completely unselfish wisdom of those words. First, we're indebted to our parents because they were responsible for bringing us into the world. Next, we're indebted to the doctors, nurses, aides, orderlies, and other hospital personnel for the part they played in making our arrival a safe and healthy one.

We're indebted to the educational structure where we learned reading, writing, and arithmetic, which are critical to our lives. It's sobering to realize that yes, somebody did have to teach Albert Einstein that two plus two equals four.

> *We all have the same amount of time, but not the same talent and ability. Those who use their time well, however, often surpass those with more ability.*

We are in debt to all the pastors, priests, and rabbis who taught us the essence of life by instructing us in the character qualities that are important to us, regardless of our chosen field of endeavor—athletics, medicine, education, business, or government.

We certainly owe a debt to people whose messages have

been encouraging and positive as well as informative and instructional. We are deeply in debt to public servants who committed their lives to service through appointed or elected offices in this great land of ours as well as to the postal worker who brings the mail, the press operators and reporters who are responsible for putting words into print, and the workers who build the highways upon which we move from one location to another.

The list is endless—which brings us back to Einstein and his quote. We have a heavy debt, and one way to repay that debt is to regularly express thanks and gratitude to the men and women who make our lives worth living. Think about it. Thank a lot of people, and you will accumulate many friends and enjoy life more.

———————

Man on phone: "No, I'm not the least bit interested." Saleswoman: "That's surprising! This exciting, new product would solve all your problems." Man: "Oh, I thought you were calling trying to collect for all the things we've already bought."

Sam Walton Was a People Person

I suppose Sam Walton has been recognized and honored by more people than just about any other businessman in this century. He truly was a unique individual, and although I never had the privilege of meeting him personally, I have met people who knew him well. I also have read what he wrote and much of what other people have written about him, and I've come to admire and respect him for the great human being he was.

Intelligently selfish people are completely unselfish because they know that it's the best way to win big-time.

Many writers focused on his phenomenal success, but Sam probably summed it up best when he said, "The reason we're successful is because we spot, we recruit, and we retain the best people." He stated emphatically, "We're in the people business." The reality is, regardless of what business we're in, since it is fueled by people, we are all in the people business. Sam also possessed a vision and tremendous commitment to bring to the most people the best product at the best price. He left no stone unturned to reach that objective. He took his business to the small towns that, at that time, were primarily shunned by other merchandising organizations.

Sam Walton was an innovator. He introduced new methods

and procedures, using all the available high technology. He communicated via satellite and called his managers once a week to get reports from them and to update them on new products and procedures they were installing. He was a hands-on leader who paid lower salaries to his executives than most companies do. However, he gave them and all his employees an opportunity to own stock in the corporation, and many of them have become wealthy as a result. He said he discovered early on that when he enriched others, he was enriched. That's a pretty good philosophy to live by. It's one that will work for all of us.

———————

A business conference is a meeting in which everyone says that there is no such thing as a free lunch while eating one.

Is There More Than One Way?

A few months before her untimely death, I spotted my daughter Suzan in my rearview mirror as I was driving to the office. Suzan worked closely with me on my newspaper column, and she, too, was headed for the office. A minute later she drove past me because she was in the fast-moving center lane while I was in the slow-moving right lane. After a short while I passed her, waving and smiling as I did so. A few blocks later she passed me again. She was grinning quite broadly as if to say, "You see, Dad, the center lane is best after all." But her triumph was short-lived; in a few more blocks I passed her.

By then we were just a few blocks from the office, and traffic was considerably heavier. Suzan missed her turn and sped past me as I turned to head for the office. Just as I pulled into my parking place, Suzan—who had taken the longer but quicker route—was pulling into hers.

The first point is, we really should not be too concerned when somebody gets ahead of us, whether in traffic or in life. In the ever-changing landscape of life,

> *Failure is not necessarily at the end of the road. Many times it is the beginning of a new and more exciting trip.*

the sun often shines on one person for a spell, then shines on another. The second point is, sometimes the shortest or easiest way is not necessarily the best or even the fastest way. We must frequently make detours to arrive at our destination. Had Suzan attempted to turn from the center lane, it might have meant disaster. Because she was flexible and willing to detour, she arrived exactly as she had planned. The third point is, we should be willing and excited to learn from the success of others. If someone is able to pass us by and arrive ahead of us, we should say, "Super good! How'd you do it?" Think about it.

Giving Congress a pay raise is like giving the captain of the Titanic *a salary increase after he hit the iceberg.* (David Evans)

Persistence Really Does Pay

*F*or eight years the struggling young writer wrote incredible numbers of short stories and articles for publication, and for eight long years they were rejected. Fortunately, he didn't give up, and for that he—and America—will always be grateful.

He spent much of his time in the navy writing a mountain of routine reports and letters. He learned how to say things eloquently, yet concisely. After his hitch in the navy, he tried desperately hard to make it as a writer, but despite those eight years and hundreds of stories and articles, he was unable to sell even one. On one occasion, however, an editor wrote an encouraging note on the rejection slip. It simply said, "Nice try."

I think you'll agree that most of us would not rate that little comment very high on the encouragement list, but it literally brought tears to the young writer's eyes. He was given new hope and continued to persist. He simply would not give up. Finally after many years of effort, he wrote a book that has deeply affected the entire world and helped him to become one of the most influential writers of the '70s. I'm speaking of Alex Haley and his book *Roots,* which was made into one of the most-watched television miniseries of all time.

> *Perseverance is very important to success. How else would two snails have made it to the ark?*

The message is clear: If you have a dream and if you really believe you have some ability that can be expressed, pursue that dream; don't give up. Hang in there! Who knows? Maybe on your next effort somebody will say, "Nice try." That might be all the encouragement you'll need. Remember, success might be just around the corner, over the next hill, or at the end of that next effort.

I'm way overdue for a promotion. I've made so many lateral moves I'm beside myself. (*Money and Business*)

Anything Can Happen—And It Often Does

One of the clichés in professional athletics is that on any given day in any given city, one professional athletic team can beat another team. Their standings in the win-loss record at that moment don't really matter. That's equally true in individual competition with players who are skilled and determined to do their best.

Kathy Horvath had every reason to believe that she would lose when she faced Martina Navratilova on May 28, 1983. Kathy was rated forty-fifth in the world; Martina was ranked number one, had won thirty-six straight matches, and had not lost a match all year. Her record in 1982 was ninety victories with only three defeats. Her defeats were to highly ranked players such as Chris Evert Lloyd and Pam Shriver. Furthermore, Kathy Horvath was only seventeen years old, and they were playing in front of sixteen thousand people.

As it often happens in such matches, Kathy got off to a fast start and won the first set 6–4. Martina came storming back in the second set and blew her off the court, winning that set 6–0.

> *The critic sees a problem to point it out and establish his authority or expertise. The coach sees a problem in order to work on it and improve it.*
>
> —Fred Smith

They started the last set, and it was truly nip and tuck. They were tied at 3–3, and Martina was serving. To everyone's surprise, Kathy, the overwhelming underdog, won the set and the match. Someone asked Kathy about her strategy, and she replied, "I was playing to win."

That's significant. Too many people play not to lose; Kathy Horvath was playing to win. I urge you to play to win.

Baseball manager Casey Stengel to catcher Joe Garagiola: "Joe, when they list all the great catchers, you'll be there listening."

Big Events Don't Always Get Big Attention

Most people are familiar with the fact that on October 8, 1871, fire broke out in Chicago and claimed more than two hundred lives and destroyed more than seventeen thousand buildings. It has been sung about, and at least one movie has been made about that Chicago fire—not to mention hundreds of articles and thousands of news mentions.

But many people do not realize that on October 8, 1871, fire also broke out in Peshtigo, Wisconsin. That blaze claimed an estimated fifteen hundred lives and scorched 1.28 million acres of timberland. Of course, the news media of the day were centered in and around Chicago, whereas Peshtigo was small and off the beaten path. Consequently, the attention was minimal. I think all of us would agree that the Peshtigo fire was significant, but because it didn't get the publicity, very few people are aware of the Peshtigo fire.

Doing ordinary things in an extraordinary way will assure you of an extraordinary future.

That's the way it frequently is in life. For example, Mother Teresa is world-famous for her incredible deeds and commitment to help those who cannot help themselves. She shuns publicity and makes public appearances only so that she can encourage people to make contributions to the cause that she dearly believes in. Literally thousands of people are doing significant things every day to help a neighbor, a homeless individual, or those who do not have fuel to heat their homes or food for their tables. These silent angels of mercy do these things because they want to do them and because they believe they are their brothers' keepers. The joy and satisfaction of doing something with no thought of recognition, reward, or return are all the pay these unsung heroes want. They do their good deeds for unselfish reasons. Without them, who knows what state of affairs our world would be in? I certainly don't, but I can guarantee you one thing—it would be much worse than it is today. Be a difference maker for others and it will make a difference in your life.

Politicians who promise you pie in the sky are going to use your dough.

Win-Win Negotiations

*V*irtually everything involves some sales or negotiation skills. Negotiations are easier if we come from a position of power—having complete confidence in our product. It's also nice to have an ace in the hole (a persuasive bargaining chip) that enables us to influence the other party in a positive way.

I love this story told in *Personal Selling Power*. When the Renault cars manufactured in France were sent to Japan, the Japanese required individual inspection of each car. On the other hand, the French allowed Japanese cars into their country on the basis of type inspection, where one vehicle picked at random represented all others of the same make. Needless to say, that was not an equitable arrangement.

French president François Mitterrand did not register a complaint. Instead, he ordered that all Japanese VCRs be inspected one at a time. He also insisted that VCRs be imported through one port in southern France. At the port were two slow-moving customs inspectors who were assigned to conduct thorough inspections of the tens of thousands of Japanese VCRs that were quickly piling up on the dock. It wasn't long before the Japanese government understood that the walls they had built and the walls the French had built in response were costing the citizens of both countries a lot of time and money. After a brief negotiation,

> *Tact is the knack of making a point without making an enemy.*

the Renault cars began to roll into Japan at a faster pace, and the VCRs resumed their normal import pace into France.

As nearly as I can tell, there was no threatening or media hoopla of any kind. The French quietly took their stand, and the Japanese quickly made the change. The negotiations were skillful, resulting in a win for both sides. Remember this basic lesson in life: If you can arrange any transaction or any agreement so that both sides win, the long-range best interests of both will be served.

———————

Chairman of the board: "To ensure your undivided attention, I'll announce at the end of the meeting the one who will write up the minutes."

"... To Help Other People ..."

I've built my life and my business on a concept, namely, that you can have everything in life you want if you will just help enough other people get what they want. Sam Walton put it this way: "I quickly learned that when I enriched others, I also enriched myself." Part of the Scout teaching is to do a good deed every day. Not long ago, I had the opportunity to help a woman who was physically unable to lift her bag and put it in the overhead compartment on an airplane. She thanked me profusely, and I laughingly said, "Well, it gave me a chance to do my good deed for the day, so I thank you." That good deed for the day is right out of what I learned as a Boy Scout. From time to time I still hear it said by people around the country. It is a marvelous philosophy.

One of the most intriguing facts of life is that when you do something nice for someone else with no thought of benefit to yourself, you end up with some significant benefits. Scientifically speaking, when you do that nice thing the brain is flooded with serotonin, the "feel-good" neurotransmitter that helps to energize us, so the practicality of the Scout Oath is significant. A *Psychology Today* study revealed that people who are active in the community doing

> *No man who is occupied in doing a very difficult thing and doing it very well ever loses his self-respect.*
> —George Bernard Shaw

things for people who can't do for themselves are physiologically energized and are able to be more successful in their own careers.

Now, I'm certain that the typical thirteen-year-old saying the Scout Oath is unaware of all of these things, but that does not lessen the benefits that the Scout receives for doing that good deed every day. Needless to say, I'm excited about Scouting, and I hope you are too. (For further information contact Boy Scouts of America under the local listing in your telephone book.)

———————

Woman to friend: "We're still working out the wedding arrangements. I want one and he doesn't." (H. Bosch)

Respond or React

*W*hen you respond to life, that's positive; when you react to life, that's negative. Example: You get sick and go to the doctor. Chances are good that after an examination, she would give you a prescription with instructions to return in several days. If, when you walk back in, the doctor starts shaking her head and says, "It looks like your body is *reacting* to the medicine; we're going to have to change it," you probably would get a little nervous. However, if the doctor smiles and says, "You're looking great! Your body is *responding* to the medication," you would feel relieved.

Yes, responding to life is good. Reacting to the incidents of life is negative—and that's bad. The next example validates that fact.

Today, there is much turmoil in the job market, and many people are losing their jobs through downsizing, mergers, and takeovers. This creates some unusual opportunities for many people. One positive from this trend is that in the last five years, according to the *Wall Street Journal,* more than fifteen million new businesses have been created, well over half of them by women. Very few of the women had any marketable skills, and all of them had great financial need. Most of the new

> *I have found that the men and women who got to the top were those who did the job they had in hand with everything they had of energy, enthusiasm, and hard work.*
>
> —Harry Truman

businesses were "trust" businesses, meaning that the women collected the money before they delivered the goods or services. The *Journal* comments that virtually none of the women have been prosecuted and jailed for failure to deliver on that trust. That's exciting!

Many of these new businesses—possibly most of them— would never have been started had not an unfortunate event occurred in the people's lives. When those events did occur and needs became obvious, the women chose to respond, and there is little doubt that many of them are better off now than they were before the "tragedy" took place.

The message is clear: If you respond to life instead of react to it, then you've got a much better chance of achieving success.

Woman to neighbor: "I have the most marvelous recipe for meat loaf! All I have to do is mention it to my husband and he says, 'Let's eat out.'"

St. John's—A College That Works

St. John's College has roughly four hundred students who attend each of the two campuses in Annapolis, Maryland, and Santa Fe, New Mexico. The administrators have the strange idea that some writers and some books are better than others, so rather than let students pick and choose, they serve the same menu to everyone—Greek, French, music, math, and science—in a four-year great books diet of Plato, Dante, Bacon, Hume, Kant, Kierkegaard, Einstein, W. E. B. Du Bois, and Booker T. Washington.

According to an article in the *American Way Magazine,* St. John's holds fast to the medieval notion that all knowledge is one and to the Renaissance man idea that a truly educated person knows a lot about a lot. Even stranger, there are no final exams, no professional training, few intercollegiate athletics, no fraternities or sororities, and almost no electives. Even more peculiar, all St. John's tutors are prepared to teach all the books from Euclid on geometry to Machiavelli on politics and Heisenberg on quantum mechanics.

St. John's forces students to bear major responsibility for their education. The teaching or

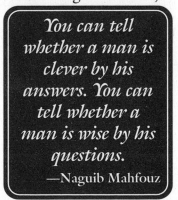

You can tell whether a man is clever by his answers. You can tell whether a man is wise by his questions.

—Naguib Mahfouz

tutoring sessions are mostly open for discussions, with every student expressing opinions, intruding ideas, and stimulating thought. They believe that we learn things together, that we don't learn alone. The books they use are terribly hard, and "you use the other people in the class to help you understand."

Question: Does it work? Answer: Yes. Seventy percent of the graduates go on to graduate school within five years of graduation, and the school ranks fifth nationally in the number of graduates earning doctorates in the humanities. Roughly 19 percent of St. John's grads become teachers or administrators. Twenty-seven percent are scattered across the professional spectrum, working in government, public affairs, computer science, engineering, and so forth. Another 20 percent find careers in business and finance, 8 percent go into law, and almost 7 percent go into the health and medical professions.

Sounds like St. John's is onto something. Maybe more schools should take that approach.

Listening to the typical politician talk is like eating bologna. You can cut it off anywhere and it's still bologna.

Be Grateful for Your Problems

*W*e all frequently deal with people who complain about the trials and tribulations of their daily lives. Life seems to be one big problem for them. I would like to take a commonsense, realistic approach and address this mind-set. If there were no problems on your job, then your employer would hire a much less capable person than you to do the routine things that don't require much thought. In the business world, those who are able to solve complex problems are the ones who are the most valuable to the employer.

Many times the problems or challenges we face force us to grow and become more capable. The runner who trains for the mile run in the Olympics by running downhill will have no chance of winning the medal. The runner who trains by running uphill is far more likely to develop the speed, mental toughness, and endurance needed to win the medal.

> *The only way to coast through life is downhill.*

The best thing that ever happened to boxer Gene Tunney was that he broke both hands in the ring. His manager felt that he could never again punch hard enough to be the heavyweight champion. Instead, Tunney decided that he would become a scientific boxer and win the title as a boxer, not a slugger. Boxing historians will tell you that he developed into one of the best boxers who ever fought. They also will tell you that as a puncher, he would not have had a chance against Jack Dempsey, who was considered by many to be the hardest hitter in heavyweight history. Tunney would never have been champion had he not had the problem of his broken hands.

Message: The next time you encounter a difficult climb, obstacle, or problem, you should smile and say, "Here's my chance to grow."

The fact that there are a lot of habitual gamblers in this world proves one thing: Men and women are the only animals that can be skinned more than once.

How Old Are You?

*Y*ou probably know some people in their forties who are "old" and others in their seventies who are "young." I say that because I believe most of the readers of this book have confidence in the 1828 Noah Webster dictionary. Not once does Webster refer to the calendar or the number of birthdays one has had. He defines *old* as "outgrown usefulness; belonging to the past; shabby; stale." I can't imagine that you would lay claim to any of these adjectives concerning the way you feel about life.

Webster says that *young* is to be "youthfully fresh in body or mind or feeling." That's the definition I like best, and at the risk of sounding immodest, I believe it describes me and the way I feel about life.

Ralph Waldo Emerson remarked, "We don't count a man's years until he has nothing else left to count." I love the Old

> *The best way to cope with change is to help create it.*
> —Robert Dole

Testament hero Caleb, who at age eighty-five asked that he be given the mountaintop where the giants were. He believed he could get rid of them, and he stated that he felt as vigorous and healthy as he had at age forty. Apparently, he was right because there are no nine-foot giants left.

Somebody observed that "a comfortable old age is the reward of a youth well-spent." This point ties into what psychiatrist Smiley Blanton says, "I have never seen a single case of senility in people, no matter how old, as long as they maintain an active interest in other human beings and in things outside of themselves." Personally speaking and relying on other sources, I don't go quite that far, but I do believe that, for example, Alzheimer's is a disease while senility, in many cases, is the direct result of a long series of wrong choices.

Follow sensible health rules and exercise on a regular basis. Continue to learn new things, fill your mind with good, clean, pure, powerful thoughts all of your life, and I believe that you can live well now and finish well.

Don't be critical of your mate's faults. It was those very defects that kept him or her from getting a better mate.

Good News in the Newspaper

*O*ver the years I've heard many people comment that they no longer read the newspaper. They say there is too much bad news and not enough good news. For that reason, I was impressed when AP and UPI carried heartwarming stories about two unusual people.

The Associated Press told the story of Dung Nguyen. When she arrived in the United States from Vietnam, she could speak only one word of English. Eight years later she graduated as valedictorian of her high school class in Pensacola, Florida. Her accomplishments were so remarkable that the president phoned to congratulate her. She was thrilled by his call, but she was even more thrilled by the opportunity America had given her.

United Press International told a quite different but equally exciting and encouraging story about Geraldine Lawhorn. Geraldine

> *Obstacles are the things we see when we take our eyes off our goals.*

was one of the older graduates of her class from Northeastern Illinois University. The unusual thing about Geraldine is that she cannot see or hear. In fact, she was only the sixth person who could not see or hear to graduate from college. When Geraldine was asked about her remarkable achievements, she replied, "We all have the same goals, but we have to go on different roads."

Setting your goals is a very personal thing, and what works for you might not necessarily work for somebody else. But one principle that worked for Dung Nguyen and Geraldine Lawhorn will work for you or anybody else. They didn't give up. Both women looked at their obstacles and saw challenges and opportunities. The exciting thing about their stories is that you can, by following their examples, finish on top as they did.

———————

An IQ test question given to a banker, an electrician, and a politician was, "What term would you use to describe the problem that results when outflow exceeds inflow?" The banker wrote, "Overdraft," the electrician wrote, "Overload," and the politician wrote, "What problem?"

"Don't Give It a Thought"

*T*he first two and a half years I was in sales, I lived in the world of peaks and valleys—with very few peaks. Every year, the last week in August, our company had a National Booster Week when we were encouraged to do nothing but sell, sell, sell. It proved to be a life-changing experience for me.

During that first National Booster Week, after I finally hit my stride, I sold more than two and a half times as much as I had ever sold in a single week. When the week ended, I drove to Atlanta, Georgia, to spend the night with Bill Cranford, who had brought me into the business. I arrived at 3:00 A.M., and for the next two and a half hours I gave Bill all the minute details of my marvelous week—a word-by-word, nonstop description of every call I had made. Bill patiently smiled, nodded his head, and said, "That's good! That's good!"

By 5:30 A.M., I realized that I had not even asked Bill how he or his business was doing. I was terribly embarrassed. I said, "Bill,

> *How people play the game shows something of their character. How they lose shows all of it.*

I'm sorry! I have just been talking about me. How are you doing?"

Bill, as only he could, graciously said, "Zig, don't give it a thought! As pleased as you are with your results this week, you're not nearly as proud as I am. You see, Zig, I recruited you, taught you the fundamentals, encouraged you when you were discouraged, counseled you, and watched you grow and mature. Zig, you will never know how I feel until you have experienced the joy of teaching, training, and developing someone else who does well."

In retrospect, I realize that was the beginning of the development of the concept on which I've built my life and career, namely, that you can have everything in life you want if you will just help enough other people get what they want. Give that philosophy a try. It works because it is the golden rule expressed in a different way.

——————————

Things change. A boy came home and told his dad he was second in class. Top place was won by a girl. "Surely, Son," said the father, "you're not going to be beaten by a mere girl." Boy: "Well, you see, Dad, girls are not nearly as mere as they used to be." (Executive Speechwriter Newsletter)

Be a Good-Finder

*F*ranklin Holmes is a volunteer chaplain working in prisons in Tennessee, Georgia, and Florida. Using a page from my book *See You at the Top,* Chaplain Holmes is teaching a program in the prisons about the importance of looking for the good in every situation. Incredibly enough, the men and women have come up with more than thirty things they like about the place where they are incarcerated. They don't like being confined, but they are, and they also understand that this is the best way to make their stay more tolerable and even beneficial.

Here's a partial list of what they like:

1. The self-help programs, church programs, and Bible studies offered them.
2. Going outside and working.
3. The store and library in the prison.
4. The yard, some of the food, and the gym.
5. Being able to go into the chapel and enjoy the peace and quiet.
6. The state movies on the weekends and some of the officers.
7. Getting incentive slips and being able to stay straight.
8. Having time to see where they went wrong and being able to use their time wisely.

> *A mistake: An event, the full benefit of which has not yet been turned to your advantage.*
>
> —Edwin Land

9. Not being looked down on in their dorms all the time.
10. Being able to work on their attitudes and develop their faith.
11. Being able to work on their goals and relationships.
12. "Doing their time" instead of "their time doing them."
13. Their job assignments, which include freedom and flexibility.
14. Their location in the mountains and foothills.
15. The library selections and the availability of the local newspaper.
16. The availability of counseling, contact visitation, and packages from home.
17. New clothing and available alterations.
18. Access to medical and dental services.
19. The training, visitation, and incentive programs.
20. Access to an updated law library.

These men and women can find thirty-eight things they like about the place where they are incarcerated. Surely, we can find many things we like about who we are, what we do, where we live, the people we live with, the opportunities life presents. Be a good-finder, and your life will be much happier.

———————————

If you expect to make it in life, remember that a spurt here and a spurt there will not make you an expert.

Stress—Good or Bad?

*T*he 1828 Noah Webster dictionary says that *stress* is "to force or drive." It is "urgency, pressure, importance." It is "focus, concentration of attention, to emphasize." When we look at the entire dictionary definition of stress, we learn that stress can be either good or bad. Too much stress will cause us to lose sleep, make us edgy and irritable, and give us high blood pressure. If we don't feel any stress, we may not be placing any significance on what we're doing. That can be as bad as too much stress. It seems that balance in our lives is the key as far as stress is concerned.

How do we handle relatively minor stressful situations (temporary increase in workload, a small overdraft at the bank, car threatening us with a repair bill, etc.) and adjust it to the proper level? This is one area where our feelings are extremely important. Most of us can sense when we're feeling too much stress, so let's look at some methods for stress reduction when relatively minor stress producers come along.

> *Properly handled, a certain amount of stress can work on our behalf.*

You need to identify the cause of stress. Is it a misunderstanding with a coworker or family member? Is it getting so involved in your responsibility that you lose your sense of perspective for the everyday facets of a balanced lifestyle? If so, what can you do about it? First, if it's a people problem, take time to talk it out. Try to put yourself in the other person's shoes. If you're wrong, admit it and apologize. You won't lose face. You'll gain respect because you have acknowledged that you're wiser today than you were yesterday. Second, find a pressure release. Take time for yourself, even if just a few minutes. Some quiet reading, a good walk, some relaxation, or a shift of scenery can work wonders. Take these steps to relieve that stress.

———————

In 1492 Columbus didn't know where he was going, had a mutinous crew, and was entirely dependent on borrowed money. Today he'd be a political candidate. (Orben's "Current Comedy")

He Got Better, Not Bitter

*O*ne of my favorite people, and certainly one of America's finest communicators, is Neal Jeffrey. Neal, as quarterback, led the Baylor Bears football team to the Southwest Conference championship in 1974. Today, he addresses many youth groups as well as adult businesspeople. He is truly one of the most humorous, sincere, and capable speakers I've ever heard.

The interesting thing is that Neal is a stutterer. However, he has chosen to make stuttering an asset, not a problem.

Now think about what you just read. A very successful quarterback and public speaker who stutters doesn't compute in the minds of most people. Neal Jeffrey has taken a negative and turned it into a positive. After speaking a few minutes, he tells

> *When (not if) troubles and problems come your way, remember that the only way to the mountaintop is through the valley.*

audiences that in case they hadn't noticed, he stutters. Then with a big smile, he says, "Sometimes I do get hung up a little bit. But don't worry. I guarantee you something's coming!" The audience invariably responds enthusiastically.

Neal is the classic example of an outstanding individual who chose to make an obstacle an asset. The obstacle has forced Neal to be more creative and to do more reading, research, and studying so he can most effectively turn that liability into an asset. Result: He got better, not bitter. He is better not in spite of his stutter, but because of his stutter. Neal has reached and is reaching goal after goal in all areas of his life. I believe that you can do the same thing.

All of us have liabilities that can hold us back or propel us forward. In most cases, the choice is ours. So, take your obstacles or liabilities, recognize and evaluate them, and then find a way to turn them into assets.

Teacher: "Greg, tell the class what is meant by compromise."
Greg: "A compromise is a deal in which two people get what neither of them wanted."

K.I.S.S.

When I started my sales career, one of the first things I was taught was to "*Keep It Simple, Salesman.*" Communicate in such a way that your message is unmistakably clear. If the message is not clear, the prospect ends up confused, and a confused person seldom takes action.

This advice can be followed in any field of endeavor. For example, in marathon running today we use sports psychologists, computerized training regimens, and state-of-the-art running shoes. Perhaps all of that is necessary if you want to win the big race. I'm not denying that these things help, but Toshihiko Seko didn't need them to win the Boston Marathon.

I was tremendously impressed when Seko won the Boston Marathon in 1981. His training program was simplicity itself, and Seko explained it with twelve words: "I run ten kilometers in the morning and twenty in the evening." At this point you probably think, *There's a catch!* But this plan enabled him to outrun the world's greatest, fastest, most gifted runners. When Seko was told that his plan seemed too simple compared to that of other marathoners, he replied, "The plan is simple, but I do it every single day, 365 days a year." Simple? Yes. Easy? No.

It is my conviction that most people fail to reach their goals not because their plans are too simple or too complicated.

> *Two sure ways to fail: Think and never do, or do and never think.*

Most people don't reach their goals because they're not committed and willing to follow their plans.

Many of our goals do not require detailed plans, but all of them require that we must follow the plan we have. Seko's plan was effective because he followed it every day. You can't get more simple than that! Follow Toshihiko Seko's example; make certain your plan to reach your goal is simple, then follow it carefully.

Recorded on a department store answering machine: "If you are calling to place an order, press 5. If you are calling to register a complaint, press 6-4-5-9-8-3-4-8-2-2-9-5-5-3-9-2. Have a good day."

Success Is a Partnership

A cliché declares that behind every successful man there is a surprised mother-in-law. In most, if not all, cases, success is a direct result of the efforts of the individual and the support and encouragement of another person or persons.

Like the fellow says, when you see a turtle on a fence post, you can rest assured that it did not get there by itself. When you see an individual climbing the success ladder and reaching the top, you know he or she did not get there entirely as a result of his or her own efforts. In virtually every case, the person had hope and encouragement from others.

Nathaniel Hawthorne is a good example. He was discouraged and had a broken heart when he went home to tell his wife, Sophia, that he was a failure because he had been fired from his job in the customhouse. Upon hearing the news, she startled him with an exuberant exclamation of joy. "Now," she said triumphantly, "you can write your book!" To that, Hawthorne responded with the question, "What are we going to live on while I am writing this book?" To his surprise and delight, she opened a drawer and drew out a substantial sum of money. "Where did you get that?" he asked. "I've always known you were a man of genius," she told him, "and I knew that someday you would write a masterpiece, so every week,

> *Many people have gone a lot farther than they thought they could because someone else thought they could.*

out of the money you gave me for housekeeping, I saved part of it. Here's enough to last us for a whole year." From his wife's trust, confidence, thrift, and careful planning came one of the classics of American literature—*The Scarlet Letter*. That story can be repeated a few thousand times—or make that a few million. It happens all the time.

If that is your story in life, I hope you're careful to give credit to those who assisted you.

Put all our congressmen together and they weigh about 96,000 pounds. It's hard to get anything that weighs 48 tons to move quickly. (Charlie "Tremendous" Jones)

The Edsel Was an Outstanding Success

𝖄ou may recall that the Edsel automobile produced by the Ford Motor Company was, in the view of the buying public, a dismal failure. Tens of millions of dollars were lost; it was the butt of numerous jokes and was soon in the graveyard of cars that did not make it.

The rest of the story, however, is quite different. You fail not when you're beaten, but when you quit. The Ford Motor Company—as you know—did not quit. As a matter of fact, out of the Edsel came incredible success. Some of the technology developed and research that followed enabled the company to produce the Mustang, which was, until that time, Ford's all-time best-seller and most profitable motorcar. From what the engineers learned from the Mustang, they were able to produce the Taurus, and for several years the Taurus has been the number one selling automobile in America.

God looks for growth, not perfection, so our objective is excellence, not perfection.

The key to all of this is that when we make a mistake—and all of us periodically do—we should make it a point to ask, What can I learn to change this temporary failure into a resounding success? That's the beginning point of doing great things. We never really reach our full potential until we've been tested and tried. Traditionally, the team that takes the toughest route to the Super Bowl, challenging and beating the toughest teams, is the one that wins the Super Bowl.

Message: When adversity is staring you in the face and you fail in an endeavor, look at it as a learning experience. That's what Ford did. That's why the Edsel was ultimately such a success in the overall scope of things. Adjust your thinking to that approach, and you will convert your "Edsels" to successes.

This country is so urbanized we think low-fat milk comes from cows on aerobic exercise. (H. A. O'Rourke)

Turning Tragedy into Triumph

*F*or many generations before this century the standard procedure for developing skilled craftsmen was for the father to teach the sons his trade. The skills necessary for the craft were passed from one generation to another. Many years ago a shoemaker was teaching his nine-year-old son his craft to prepare him for life. One day, an awl fell from the shoemaker's table and tragically put out the eye of his nine-year-old son. Without the medical knowledge and expertise of today, the son ended up losing not only that eye, but the other one as well.

His father put him in a special school for people without sight. At that time they were taught to read by using large carved wooden blocks. The blocks were clumsy, awkward to handle, and required a considerable amount of time to learn. The shoemaker's son, however, was not content only to learn to read. He knew there must be an easier, better way. Over the years, he devised a new reading system for people who were blind by punching dots into paper. To accomplish his objective, the shoemaker's son

> *Each of us will one day be judged by our standard of life, not by our standard of living; by our measure of giving, not by our measure of wealth; by our simple goodness, not by our seeming greatness.*
>
> —William Arthur Ward

used the same awl that had blinded him. His name was Louis Braille.

The saying is still true: It's not what happens to you; it's how you handle what happens to you that counts. I love what President Reagan said about his first term in office: "Since I came to the White House I got two hearing aids, a colon operation, skin cancer, a prostate operation and I was shot." He paused. "I've never felt better in my life." I believe you will agree that attitude will propel you farther than bemoaning unfortunate incidents in your life. Give it a try. Take the advice of Helen Keller, who said, "If the outlook is not good, try the uplook. It's always good."

———————

One commuter to another: "Actually, my mother-in-law and I have a lot in common. We both wish my wife had married someone else." (H. Bosch)

Yesterday's Impossibles

I remember the media coverage that accompanied Edmund Hillary's feat of being the first person to scale Mount Everest. He became an instant celebrity, even though he had failed in his first effort and left five of his guides dead on the mountainside. England recognized his tremendous effort by giving him the highest honor awarded a foreigner, a knighthood. Years later he was back in the headlines when his son climbed to the peak of Mount Everest, and father and son held a radio-phone conversation.

Today, according to the government of Nepal, climbers often reach the peak of Mount Everest. As a matter of fact, a one-day record of thirty-seven people reaching the summit of Mount Everest has been reported. Seven teams arrived within a half-hour period and created a climbers' traffic jam. Yes, yesterday's impossibles often become tomorrow's standards.

On September 6, 1995, one of the world's unbreakable records was broken. I speak of the "Iron Man" stunt of Lou Gehrig, who played in 2,130 consecutive baseball games. Gehrig's record was thought to be unbreakable, but Cal Ripken broke that record and is extending that streak to make it even more impossible. Another record considered unbreakable was the number of hits Ty Cobb had gotten, but several years ago Pete Rose broke that unbreakable record. Today, twelve-year-old

> *The best time to do something significant is between yesterday and tomorrow.*

girls are swimming faster than Johnny Weissmuller swam when he was the Olympic gold medal winner.

Most of us get excited when we read about superhuman achievements, but something that is much more important is breaking our personal best records for accomplishments. Achieving better grades, a better work record, a better record of "being nice," and a host of other records will make you a better person in the most important game of all—the game of life.

———————————

Football referee Jim Tunney says, "My definition of a fan is a guy who screams at you from the 60th row of the bleachers because he thinks you missed a holding call in the center of the interior line, then after the game can't find his car in the parking lot."

Eating an Elephant

*I*t's been around for years, but the statement that you can eat an elephant one bite at a time is as true as ever. It's also true that you can benefit humankind and change the lives of countless others a little bit at a time.

One of the most heartwarming stories I've heard in years is that of Oseola McCarty from Hattiesburg, Mississippi. She is eighty-eight years old and has spent a lifetime washing, ironing, and mending clothes. The clothes were worn at parties she never attended, weddings to which she was never invited, and graduations that she was not privileged to see. Her needs in life were extremely simple. She didn't mind living in a small house and economizing in every possible way—including cutting the toes out of shoes if they did not fit right. Her pay over the decades was small and mostly in dollar bills and change, but she saved consistently and recently donated $150,000 to finance scholarships for African-American students at the University of Southern Mississippi. The impact of

> *When you're confronted with challenges, instead of starting thoughts or sentences with, "The problem is . . ." change it to, "The opportunity for change is . . . ," or "The opportunity for improvement is . . . ," or "The opportunity for growth is. . . ."*

her gift has been incredible. She has been identified as the most unselfish person anyone knows. The business leaders of Hattiesburg matched the $150,000, and the $300,000 is being used for the scholarships.

Ms. McCarty is still stunned at the amount of attention she is getting from the media and the number of people who come by to see her. She has only one request and hope: that she will be privileged to attend the graduation of at least one of the students who received his or her college education as a result of her generosity. She wishes she had been able to get a college education herself, but says she was always "too busy." It's her hope now that her "busyness" will enable others to get the education she never had.

Fact: It's not how much you have but how well you use what you have that counts. I encourage you to follow the Oseola McCarty example and help others achieve success. You will feel even better about their success than they do.

A psychiatrist's ad in the local paper: "Satisfaction guaranteed or your mania back." (John W. Perritt)

It Takes Courage

*J*anet Carroll has courage in abundance, and she is making a difference and providing encouragement to people all over America by calling to our attention unsung heroes who usually are not recognized but who surround us, dressed in a thousand different outfits. Janet Carroll is also a woman of audacity, commitment, imagination, and a willingness to go the extra mile.

She conceived an idea to bring to the public's attention some exciting things happening in our country. She chose to concentrate on some quiet people who shun the spotlight while making America a better place to live. She quit her job, borrowed $27,000 on her credit cards, and became the writer/producer/director/salesperson/entrepreneur/organizer/creator/motivator for the *Unsung Heroes* television program. Her first program aired on December 23, 1991, and for three years was seen in prime time, six or seven times each year.

> *You conquer negative thinking with positive thinking, which is more than the little red engine that repeated, "I think I can, I think I can." It's exploring why and searching for resources. It's knowing you're right. It's switching the reverses of life into high gear and making them positive.*

In retrospect, Janet Carroll says that had she known then what she knows today, she probably would not have started the program. Consider the odds: No money, single mother, no experience producing a television show, and she had to go against the pros and moneyed people who have unlimited budgets, using the latest technology to produce their shows.

The impact the show has had on Janet and many others is substantial, including a cameraman who observed that he feels very "important" standing behind the camera filming important people. "But," he said, "with these unsung heroes I fully recognize that they really are the heroes and that I'm privileged to be filming them." Yes, Janet Carroll was and is a difference maker—and so are you, so make it a positive difference.

———————

I was going to enroll in an assertiveness training class but my wife said I didn't need it. (Frank Hughes)

If the Decision Is Wrong, Change It

Carol Farmer was an unhappy schoolteacher who realized after only two semesters of teaching that the education field wasn't for her. Despite her considerable investment of time and effort to become a teacher, she recognized that it wasn't her calling. But what else could she do? Her dream had always been to be a designer, so she set a goal to become one. Part of her goal was to make more money designing the first year than she had made teaching. She had earned $5,000 as a first-year teacher. As a first-year designer she earned $5,012, reaching her first goal.

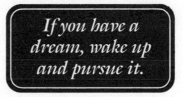

If you have a dream, wake up and pursue it.

She accepted a job with one of her clients for $22,000 a year, more than four times what she was making two years earlier. Shortly thereafter, she was offered a raise to $35,000, but her dreams had expanded and she turned it down to start her own company. She earned more than $100,000 her first year—twenty times more than she made less than ten years previously and five times more than she earned the year before. In 1976, Carol Farmer formed the Doody Company, and in the next three years billed more than $15 million. Her staff increased from six to two hundred. She has gained considerable recognition for her accomplishments and has shared her business success with scholars at Harvard University.

Too often people see obstacles as roadblocks instead of opportunities. Carol took that calculated risk—which most successful people do (it takes courage to make the start, commitment to keep going, and persistence to get there). There is merit in calculated risk, but I'm not talking about gambling. Successful people don't take blind chances. They calculate their odds, which is what Carol Farmer did. In the process, she turned the disappointment and unhappiness of one career into happiness, creativity, and profit in a different career. I encourage you to join Carol Farmer in approaching obstacles and disappointments creatively.

Money won't buy happiness, but it will pay the salaries of a huge research staff to study the problem. (Bill Vaughn)

It's Not What You Don't Have

You've heard it many times: "Life is what you make it." Or we could put it in a slightly different way, as my friend Ty Boyd does, and say, "You can't change the cards life has dealt you, but you can determine the way you'll play them." That's the philosophy Wendy Stoeker decided to live by. When she was a freshman at the University of Florida, Wendy placed third in the girls' state diving championship. At that point she was swimming in the number two spot on the highly competitive Florida swim team and carrying a full academic load.

Wendy Stoeker certainly sounds like an accomplished, happy, positive, well-balanced coed, capable of making life whatever she wishes it to be, doesn't she? Well, you're right when you say that's what she was and is. The fact is, she already has made life what she wants it to be, even though she was born without arms.

> *Circumstances can either make us or break us. The choice is ours.*

Despite having no arms, Wendy enjoys bowling and water-skiing, and she types more than forty-five words a minute. Wendy doesn't look down at what she does not have. She looks up at what she does have. The reality is that if all of us would use what we have and not worry about what we don't have, we would be able to accomplish infinitely more in our lives.

The message is this: Follow the example of Wendy Stoeker. Think positively about what you want in life. Determine to use what you have, regardless of the obstacles you might face. If you do that, you will make your life more exciting, rewarding, and productive.

———————————

Many people itch for what they want, but they won't scratch for it.

Learn to Say Yes

*W*e truly live in a hurry-hurry world, and in this day of two-working-parent families we never have enough time to do the things we want and need to do. One of these want-to-/need-to-do things is to spend more time with our children. Unfortunately, time constraints make it easier for us to automatically respond with a no when our children ask for little things. Solution: In an article published in *Better Families,* Dr. Kay Kuzma offers some practical approaches we can use. She suggests we can say yes on many occasions, and it's more effective because it also teaches valuable lessons. For example, the child might ask, "Am I going to get to watch my favorite television show tonight?" The parents have a chance to say, "Yes, as soon as you have dried the dishes and put them away," or "Yes, as soon as you have called Sally and apologized for your behavior this afternoon."

This approach changes you in the child's eyes from being a person who wants to deny him or her a pleasure to a parent who is interested in helping that child perform in a better, more mature way. The teenager might ask to use the car the next morning to run a few errands and go to the park. You can say, "Yes, as soon as you wash it and if you will stop by the service station and fill it with gas on your way home." This way you're teaching your child responsibility. You're saying yes to a reasonable request, and you're also displaying a sense of trust in your child.

> *It is not a disgrace to lack a degree, but it is a disgrace not to be educated.*

Dr. Kuzma also points out that when a child asks, "May I have dessert?" you can say, "Yes, as soon as you have finished your salad or vegetables." This way you are attaching a small reward to a fulfilled responsibility. The child ends up with the temporary pleasure and some long-term benefits. Practice Dr. Kuzma's suggestions, and you will have taken a giant step toward raising a positive, courteous, responsible child.

_____

Any marriage is in trouble when a man shows his worst side to his better half.

Is It a Problem or an Opportunity?

*R*andy Males is a furniture salesman. In furniture stores the salespeople alternate with their "ups." (They take turns serving customers as they come in the store or "come up.") One day a fellow salesperson, muttering under his breath, said, "I can't sell people like that!" Randy asked what the problem was, and the salesman told him that the man could not see or hear and the wife could see and hear only a little. The salesman emphatically stated that he would not waste his time trying to sell them and he would not allow them to be counted as his "up." Randy asked if it would be okay if he talked with the couple. The response was, "Yes, if you want to waste your time."

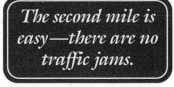

The second mile is easy—there are no traffic jams.

Randy approached the customers from the front because the woman could make out forms and things held directly in front of her. He spoke to them, and the woman signed to him that she was deaf. Randy took a pad and in big letters wrote, "Be right back." He returned with a large writing pad and "talked" with the couple using the pad. The couple left with a sizable purchase and huge smiles on their faces. The next day Randy received a call from the translation service for the deaf, thanking him for his courtesy. Randy was pleased but quickly pointed out that he was no saint. He was a salesman willing to go the extra mile.

Since that time, several of the couple's friends have come in and purchased furniture from Randy. Because he went the extra mile, Randy turned one salesman's problem into his opportunity.

I share this story with considerable pleasure because the message has real value and because Randy, a former ditchdigger, was inspired by my brother, the late Judge Ziglar. The message is clear. Be nice to people. Render service to those who need it most, and benefit yourself in the process.

Isn't it interesting that no matter what happens, we will discover a large number of people who "knew it would"?

About the Author

Zig Ziglar is chairman of the Zig Ziglar Corporation, whose goal is to help people more fully utilize their physical, mental, and spiritual resources. Hundreds of corporations worldwide use his books, videos, audiotapes, and courses to train their employees. Ziglar is one of the most sought-after motivational speakers in the country. He travels around the world delivering his message of humor, hope, and enthusiasm to audiences of all kinds and sizes. He is the author of many books, including *See You at the Top*, which has sold more than 1.5 million copies worldwide, and *Over the Top*.

Also from Zig Ziglar
and Thomas Nelson Publishers

Over the Top (Revised and Updated)
Culminating more than twenty years of experience since he wrote his best-seller *See You at the Top*, the revised and updated edition of this book is packed with on-target advice for maximum success and happiness. (ISBN 0-7852-7119-8)

Over the Top—Nelson Audio Library Edition
As only the dean of motivational speakers can, Ziglar presents the life-changing material from *Over the Top* to an enthusiastic live audience. (ISBN 0-7852-7973-3)